Real Estate Investing for the Utterly Confused

Real Estate Investing for the Utterly Confused

Lisa Moren

McGraw-Hill

New York   Chicago   San Francisco   Lisbon   London
Madrid   Mexico City   Milan   New Delhi   San Juan
Seoul   Singapore   Sydney   Toronto

The McGraw·Hill Companies

1 2 3 4 5 6 7 8 9 0   DOC/DOC   0 9 8 7 6

ISBN 0-07-147234-7

This publication is designed to provide accurate and authoritative information in regard to the subject matter covered. It is sold with the understanding that the publisher is not engaged in rendering legal, accounting, or other professional service. If legal advice or other expert assistance is required, the services of a competent professional person should be sought.

—From a Declaration of Principles Jointly Adopted by a Committee of the American Bar Association and a Committee of Publishers and Associations

McGraw-Hill books are available at special discounts to use as premiums and sales promotions, or for use in corporate training programs. For more information, please write to the Director of Special Sales, Professional Publishing, McGraw-Hill, Two Penn Plaza, New York, NY 10121–2298. Or contact your local bookstore.

 This book is printed on recycled, acid-free paper containing a minimum of 50% recycled de-inked paper.

Library of Congress Cataloging-in-Publication Data

Moren, Lisa.
    Real estate investing for the utterly confused / by Lisa Moren.
      p. cm.
    Includes index.
    ISBN 0-07-147234-7 (alk. paper)
    1. Real estate investment—Handbooks, manuals, etc. I. Title.

HD1382.5.M6694 2006
332.63'24—dc22   2006013616

Contents

Preface

Thank you for investing in yourself to learn more about investing in real estate! My objective is to give you the knowledge you need to make decisions about what type of real estate you want to buy, how to negotiate for it and buy it, get it financed, manage it if you desire, and sell it when you're ready. Look at this program as the beginning of your continuing education in real estate investing.

I have been investing in real estate since 1978. Some deals were winners, others—well, they were not so good. In this book you will get the benefit of my 28-plus years of experience, plus stories from other very successful investors. This knowledge will be your foundation to help you make decisions for your future investments.

It doesn't matter whether you do real estate full-time, part-time, or just one time. It doesn't matter what your education level is. With the right knowledge and discipline, you can achieve success in buy/sell or buy/hold real estate. This book shows you how and gives you an action plan to get started as soon as you're ready.

I wrote *Real Estate Investing for the Utterly Confused* for those who go to seminars, buy everyone's products, and then leave them on the shelf, unopened and unused. I wrote it for those who are looking for creative techniques to help them find, fund, or manage property. And I wrote it for those who just need a good refresher course.

To get the most out of this program, you must be familiar with basic real estate vocabulary. If you're confused or uncertain about any of the terms you see here, a good resource is www.homeglossary.com. This site consists of a comprehensive dictionary of over 10,000 construction and real estate terms, ranging from terms that are basic to those that are extremely specific. It is a useful Web site for both novice and experienced real estate investors.

It is my hope that *Real Estate Investing for the Utterly Confused* will make a difference in your real estate investments and wealth accumulation.

Real Estate Investing for the Utterly Confused

CHAPTER 1

Why Real Estate?

Do I Need to Read This Chapter?

➡ You want to learn how to successfully invest in real estate.

➡ You want a hedge against inflation.

➡ You want to build retirement income.

➡ You're looking for a conservative approach to investing in real estate.

Investing in Real Estate

Those of you who have purchased this book have different reasons for investing in real estate. Some of you need supplemental income to meet current financial obligations. Others may be trying to grow a retirement nest egg. Or you may just be interested in investing as a hobby. The one thing you have in common is that you want to be successful when you invest in real estate. I will do my best to help you do just that.

I hope to help you understand how investing in real estate can be a solid means of protecting your future. Why real estate? Consider these reasons:

- Real estate values have withstood the test of time. In the late 1970s and early 1980s, interest rates were in the teens. Values plummeted. Perhaps many of you don't remember this or were not even born yet! Today, interest rates are holding at around 6 percent, and the value of real estate has quadrupled. Just about every region in the country has seen tremendous growth over the past 10 years or so.

- An appreciation rate of 3 to 5 percent per year is not uncommon in investment properties. Compare this to your 1 percent money market account. In my opinion, a slow and steady increase in growth is just fine.

- Think of your down payment versus your return. If I put 5 percent down on a property and it goes up the next year at a 5 percent rate, I have made a 100 percent return on my initial investment. Over the long term, that is truly enough.

- Properties are a hedge against inflation. If you put money in your savings account, it will grow, but in the end you'll lose to inflation. Not so with real estate. Once a property price is locked in, value typically grows at or above the rate of inflation.

- You can build your portfolio by using existing real estate investments as leverage to finance other purchases. You can refinance one rental to buy another. Now that is building your portfolio!

- You can build your retirement income. If you're interested in purchasing properties for the long term, the income and cash flow you receive from these properties will help build future income. My tenants help pay off the properties I buy, giving me free and clear income for life.

- No matter what the circumstances, you can always make money with real estate investments.

- Low volatility. I know many investors who have made a fortune in the stock market. I also know many people who have lost their shirt. Real estate, overall, is a safe, secure investment.

- There is a pretty good chance that many of us will never see a Social Security benefit check, or if we do, that it won't be enough to live on. By investing in income-producing assets, you have the ability to control your own destiny. And isn't that what we all want?

Get Started

 We've posed seven categories of questions for you to consider as you decide what your investment strategy should be, with accompanying comments. As you answer them, take your family and your outside interests into account.

1. What is your present financial situation? Are you gainfully employed? An entrepreneur, a retiree? Is your income in today's dollars covering your expenses? Answer these questions with total honesty.

2. What are the financial goals or obligations that you need to meet before you retire? Are you taking care of a parent? Do you have young children you want to support through college? Are you helping to support an adult child with a family? These are real situations that don't just take care of themselves. Give these issues thoughtful consideration. This is you spending your money; you need to plan for wealth accumulation in your retirement.

3. How much investment capital do you have to get started or to keep going? Include your IRAs and old 401(k)s in the analysis.

4. How many years remain until you intend to live off retirement income? There is no such thing as a gold watch anymore, so be realistic.

5. What annual income will you need to retire? A good estimate would be 70 percent of your current income. Of course, if you plan to travel extensively, make it a higher estimate than if you plan to putter around the garden in your paid-off home.

6. How many years do you expect this income to last? This is a tough one, because people live much longer these days. Look at your family history as a guide.

7. How much risk are you willing to take today to accomplish your goals in the future? This is one of the most important questions you need to answer for yourself. A lot of us are just not risk-takers. Many people leave money sitting in a savings or money market account because they are afraid they'll lose it if they invest it any other way. The answer to this question will clarify what type of property you should be looking for, whether you buy/sell or buy/hold, and what type of investment growth you will feel comfortable with.

Developing Your Investment Strategy

Each of us has needs and objectives we want to accomplish. When it comes to real estate, our investments are the vehicles that get us to our goals. Some of us start out with zero dollars to invest. Others may have inherited money from an estate or built a net worth through hard work and wise investments. Where are you in the spectrum?

Once you've assessed your situation, develop your own personal investment strategy. The Quick Tip below, one of many you will encounter in this book, is an example of a conservative approach you can work from.

Quick Tips

The conservative approach to real estate investing:

· Evaluate trends that affect the area's economic strengths and weaknesses. When you see weakness, don't buy—you will be too nervous. Lease option or use other creative strategies to tie up property long enough for the market to turn.

· If you detect signs of an upturn, start to invest.

· When prices are so high that you can't afford to buy any longer, fix up what you have and resell for a profit, or trade it if you don't want the tax consequence.

· You always need to be "in the market" and know the real estate market where you live. By learning all of the investment strategies discussed in this book, you will have the flexibility and comfort level to know what to use and how to structure deals to make money.

✓ Evaluate your financial situation.
✓ Consider your financial goals and obligations.
✓ How much risk are you willing to take?
✓ Evaluate the economic trends of the area you're considering.
✓ Stay "in the market."

CHAPTER 2

The Right Property Type for the Right Time

Do I Need to Read This Chapter?

→ You don't know what types of property to consider.

→ You want to avoid costly mistakes.

→ You've decided on your investment goals.

→ You've got a strategy to reach them.

Choosing Properties

Once you have decided on your investment goals and a strategy to reach them, spend some time deciding what types of properties best suit your purposes. Each type of property offers different profit potential, and learning what to look for and when to buy are crucial to your success.

Careful planning at this stage will help you avoid costly mistakes and a lot of regret. Understand that every investor makes some mistakes along the way; the purpose of this manual is to help you avoid some of the most common ones! Most investors focus on one type of property and learn that market very well. Let's look at the advantages and drawbacks of each type.

Single Family Houses

These have the advantage of being easier to resell than, say, apartments or condos. Also, the initial capital outlay is obviously much less than for a multiunit complex or a commercial property. Some investors get their start by buying a home and living in it for a year. Then they convert it to a rental and purchase another home to move into, building their portfolio slowly but economically. With single family homes, you have the additional advantage of being able to have a mix of locations of your rental properties, instead of having all units under one roof. This helps spread your risk in an economic downturn.

Houses, however, do not appreciate in value as much as multiple units, and if not purchased correctly, they can produce negative cash flow. They tend to be more expensive to upkeep than multiple units. For example, a multiple unit dwelling may have one heating system to service four units, whereas each single family house has its own. If you owned four houses with four cranky heating systems, you could incur more costs and spend more time and money on maintenance checks.

Condos and Town Homes

These can generate solid revenue, but never purchase a condo or a town home without first becoming intimately acquainted with its homeowner association's bylaws. Make sure you understand all covenants and restrictions to avoid headaches (and possible lawsuits) later.

Homeowner associations are naturally interested in maintaining optimal value, so many will not even allow a rental, or will allow only a certain percentage of units to be set aside for rental. Keep in mind that association and assessment fees are not fixed. An assessment fee is levied when some improvements or repairs are needed, and this can easily ruin your investment budget. You have no control over what the association does with your money, nor do you have any control over any increase in fees. Finally, in a down market, these properties carry higher risk on resale.

Monopoly on the Boardwalk

Fourteen years ago my mother bought an efficiency condo in a high rise on the New Jersey shore. She paid $150,000 and took out a 20-year loan. In addition to her mortgage payment, taxes, and insurance, her monthly condo fee is $250 to cover building security and maintenance.

Five years ago the area started to change. Her condo value dropped to $65,000, roughly what she still owed. Three years ago the homeowner's association assessed each unit in the building $20,000 over and above her $250 per month condo fee.

When she was hit with this assessment, Mom became frantic. She is a widow on a fixed income, as are many of her neighbors. I called a local realtor and asked to have market comps prepared. I learned that her unit was valued at $48,000. Now, she actually owed more on her mortgage than the condo was worth! She was upside down on her mortgage.

Failure to pay off the $20,000 assessment would result in a lien being placed against her condo. Worse, at this writing the monthly fee is scheduled to go up another $100. Mom ended up getting a home equity loan to pay off the assessment. This became a financial strain. She continued to hold onto the property, even though she could have sold.

In the last two years, property values came back. She recently sold the condo for double what she paid for it. Mom got lucky because the market bounced back to the point where she was able to pay off her loans and still make a decent profit.

Don't Forget

Condos and town homes can be good investments, but only if you can profitably absorb inflationary costs and unpredictable assessments. Be aware and buy right!

Seasonal Units

Baby boomers have a lot of accumulated wealth. Many of them have speculated in buying vacation homes in "sun and fun" spots as good investments for seasonal rentals. They buy them as a getaway destination as well. If done right, these rentals can offset your total annual mortgage and maintenance costs, but be careful. Factors over which you have no control, such as weather and the economy, can effectively shoot down your investment plan.

A good example is the Front Range of the Rocky Mountains, where I lived from 1990 to 2003. Properties in places like Vail and Aspen have skyrocketed in value over the past two decades because they offer breathtaking beauty and world-class skiing. But if an investor bought into one of these communities a couple of years ago hoping to meet expenses through collecting rent from well-heeled skiers, he would be lost. Two of the driest winters on record have occurred in the past three years, and the dwindling snow on the slopes has meant less tourists.

Before you buy, consider whether you can afford to have long intervals with no renters. Also, become familiar with IRS regulations on deducting losses while renting out personal vacation homes. The law is very specific and rather complicated.

Seasonal Units . . . Rent or Buy?

Several years ago Don and his wife decided to invest in a condo at a major Colorado ski resort in a good location near the slopes and close to a convenience store.

They paid $295,000 for the unit and then paid more to furnish it tastefully. They expected to spend a few weekends a year at the condo, but the main purpose was to rent it out during ski season to pay the mortgage.

They soon learned it is very difficult and expensive to rent out a ski resort property. Web site or magazine advertising cost a fortune. They turned to the resort's property management company. This meant paying a 55 percent management fee, which included the cleaning and maintenance of the unit, snow removal, and a set fee for on-call emergencies.

The first winter, the unit was rented out three times. Obviously, this did not cover the mortgage payments. Don realized that since there were so many rental units to choose from, his condo seldom came up on the list. Today the property is worth around $500,000—a good gain on their initial investment. However, they have never had a positive rental year. In fact, they have never had a year that paid their homeowner's fees.

By the way, Don still owns the property and has talked to us about buying into it for a certain number of weeks. For the cost of ownership, I could rent a unit for a month in the winter (high season) and still be ahead 30 years later.

Don't Forget

If you want a seasonal resort-type property, keep in mind that this is a different kind of investment—one for you to enjoy.

Duplexes

These have a lot of appeal if you value living on one side of your house and having a renter on the other side helping you pay your mortgage. For this reason, they're very popular as first-time investments. However, as straight rentals that are not owner-occupied, they have some drawbacks.

For example, with duplexes, most investors have the tenants maintain the landscaping. More often than not, though, one tenant is more responsible about this than the other. Because duplex living is less anonymous than apartment living, if side-by-side tenants don't get along, headaches ensue for the landlord.

Most professional real estate investors pass over duplexes in favor of larger units. From a resell perspective, however, duplexes sell like hotcakes, because there is always that investor out there who wants an owner-occupied arrangement. They also make great flipper properties and rehab properties.

Dan Dumps the Duplex

Dan and Mary bought a duplex in St. Petersburg, Florida. They lived on one side and rented out the other side to a nice elderly couple. This arrangement lasted until Dan and Mary started their family. Soon they needed a single family home.

They decided to keep the duplex, renting out both sides. This would help pay off the mortgage more quickly and provide extra income for their growing family.

Dan rented the duplex to a likable young couple with a young child and a dog. This is when problems began. The dog was destructive. He dug holes around the property and wreaked havoc with the elderly couple's vegetable garden. The elderly couple complained. Twice Dan talked with his tenants about their dog and alluded to eviction if the dog could not be controlled. However, there was nothing in the lease that addressed the dog, and the couple refused to get rid of him.

One day the elderly couple was coming home from the grocery store, and the dog chased them from their car to their front door. That was it. After living there happily over 10 years, they gave Dan 30 days notice and moved. Dan lost the best tenants he ever had.

Now Dan had a vacancy. He tried to rent the property, but couldn't find a tenant. Eventually, he sold the duplex at a loss just to get rid of it. As far as he is concerned, he will never be a landlord again.

What really went wrong was that Dan, with his full-time work and family obligations, did not have time for property management. He also learned the hard way the importance of carefully screening prospective tenants.

Don't Forget

Duplexes are an excellent way to start building a solid real estate portfolio, but you must be able to perform effectively as a landlord.

Three- and Four-Unit Buildings

Four-unit buildings are a bit more profitable than triplexes, because they can be financed with the same type of loan. Also, they may not cost much more to buy, but are more profitable per unit. They are manageable enough for a new investor.

When buying a multiple-unit building, you're more likely to deal with a real estate professional than a private individual. To protect yourself, learn all you can about property. Evaluate such things as:

- Incomplete expense reports
- Physical defects in the property
- Building code violations
- Neighborhood positioning
- Desirability of location
- Exaggerated income reports
- Expiring leases
- Liens on the property
- Appraised value
- Comparable market properties
- Any other data you can compile

The nice thing about a triplex or a quad is that you can buy it like a house. If you plan to live in the building, you can find lenders who offer loans with low down payments. Interest rates on buildings that house two to four units also can be as low as those of single family houses. Plus, you can live in one unit and take advantage of depreciation and other write-offs for the other units.

Apartment Buildings: Five or More Units

The logic here is that the larger the building, the more the earning potential. However, bigger buildings can also bring bigger headaches. Here are some points to consider before entering this market:

Major Trader

Major Trader started buying four-plexes in 1978. He was 28 years old and working at a liquor store. His first building cost $19,900. He moved into one unit and took six months, mostly on weekends, to fix up the other three units. He immediately rented out each unit as he finished rehabbing it, and kept everything rented for a year. He then sold the four-plex for $40,000 and bought another for $29,900 in the same neighborhood. This building also needed work. He quit his job and worked full-time on his own fixing up his units.

Today he is 54 years old, owns over 100 four-plexes, and hasn't worked a day job since the liquor store. His simple plan and constant deal-making has made him a multimillionaire. He only buys and trades four-plexes.

- You will compete for properties with experienced real estate investors.
- You'll need to have a lot more money on hand for your down payment.
- From the lender's perspective, the property will stand on its own.
- You may get more flexible financing if you can find a lender who understands commercial buildings, internal rates of return, net operating income, etc.
- You many have to hire professional management to manage the building.

Multifamily housing is in high demand in many parts of the country today. Working people scramble to find affordable, well-maintained apartments in decent neighborhoods. An apartment building is one of the best investments there is, provided you have cash reserves and a good understanding of multifamily real estate and zoning laws.

Mobile Homes and Home Parks

These have both advantages and drawbacks. They produce great cash flow, and the tenant pool for the properties is larger than for other types of housing. Also, very little down payment is required. Prices, however, are not stable. Mobile homes depreciate in value, and they're treated as personal property and not real property when land is not associated with the deal. They are viewed negatively in some parts of the country as representing neighborhood blight, so know the mind-set of the community before you invest.

Investing in mobile homes?... it's up to you. I no longer invest in them. That does not mean you shouldn't.

Mobile Home Madness

Years ago, I lived in a part of North Carolina where mobile homes were more popular then single family houses. Due to a private mortgage I held that went into foreclosure, I ended up owning a mobile home park. What a cash cow! I rented the spaces for $70 per month, and soon decided to start buying my own mobile homes and putting them on the spaces to rent as a package.

I never paid more than $2,000 per unit. In addition to the monthly rent for the lot, I charged $250 to $500 for the home. In most cases, I put the home on a four-year rent-to-own plan. I would never sell the lots.

This is a great way to accumulate both cash flow and monthly income, but I advise you to live near the park. Trying to manage a park long distance is a hassle. I sold my park to a doctor who put 40 percent down, and I owner-financed it at 14 percent for five years. Good deal for me, great deal for him, since he still owns the park today.

Don't Forget

To a buyer of a mobile home, the number-one concern is that monthly payment. Price and terms are not as important. If the monthly payment is affordable, you will have no problem selling your mobile homes. Most investors structure terms to meet the borrower's needs.

Quick Tips

Pension plan tip: You can also have your self-directed IRA or self-directed 401(k) invest in these properties.

Vacant Land

Before you buy a parcel of vacant—that is, raw—land, first determine its highest and best use. You should figure out its most profitable use so that the land can produce the greatest return over a period of time.

Vacant Land . . . One Investor's Riches

Ken lives in New Mexico. Thirty years ago, he purchased tens of thousand of acres of raw land, meaning no utilities or water, in southern Colorado, close to the New Mexico border. He paid less than $20 per acre.

His entire business is selling vacant land to people who eventually want to live in the middle of nowhere. He has a billboard advertising his land: "$99 down, $99 per month. Call Ken." This is the only marketing Ken does.

Many of his customers are truck drivers passing through who see his billboard ad, look at this land full of sagebrush with distant views of the mountains, and decide to buy into the fantasy that one day this land will be worth some money. Ken has sold thousands of acres, all owner-financed. His initial investment was returned in less than three years. Just imagine the income he's made off the paper in the past 27 years. And he still has land for sale.

Improved Lots

Many investors like to buy improved lots. Their aim is to pick them up at bargain prices and then hold them just long enough to resell them to builders or developers for premium prices. Also, seller financing with a fairly low down payment is typical. Improved lots are generally more attractive for resale than raw land.

Office Buildings

The current glut of vacant office space in most major metropolitan areas makes investing in this type of real estate risky. This is not an easy first investment. If you decide you want to buy an office building, make sure you do a thorough tenant-analysis first. What kind of tenants are they? Are their leases almost up? The longer the lease, the safer the cash flow.

Specialty Investments: Mini-Warehouses and Storage Units

The key to succeeding with this type of investment is location. What do university areas have in common with retirement communities? They both have populations of people who need to store their "stuff." What if you found a community with both a large retirement population and a sizable student population? Bingo! You could strike it rich! But check competition and price carefully. What is your real return?

Get Started

Success with Storage Units

Success in the ministorage business, as with most other kinds of real estate, depends upon location. You must be located in an area where a lot of the population has "excess baggage." That is, college towns where students need to stash extra gear, growth areas where people relocating need to store their stuff before choosing a permanent home, or a retirement community where seniors are not ready to part with all their possessions in a downsizing move.

Before you decide that your town needs another ministorage facility, look at the existing competition. Figure what your costs of buying (or building) and maintaining these units will be, and add in the cost of a caretaker to oversee the facility. If your net return exceeds what you can earn in other real estate, go for it. This money-making idea caught on years ago, but it still may make a good investment in your part of the country. Do your due diligence.

Location, Location, Location . . .

Several years ago Cecil and a partner built a 300-unit ministorage facility in Mississippi. They hired a caretaker to manage the facility, which is computerized to lock tenants out of their units if they're late with the rent.

At the time, in addition to having the perfect location, Cecil had no competition. He got anywhere from $35 to $70 per unit per month. His facility was always full, with a waiting list of people wanting to rent.

In the last few years, however, several more ministorage facilities have gone up in the area. Cecil is still making money, but it has become more difficult to keep his units fully rented. He says he would not build units in this location today.

Quick Tips

Pension plan tip: You can also have your self-directed IRA or self-directed 401(k) invest in these properties. Many partners will form an LLC and buy into to storage facilities.

Shopping Centers

These investments are not for the weak-hearted! You will need knowledge and lots of money, not just for the center, but for the city and county that govern the center. Mostly partnerships and corporations enter this market. There are companies that do nothing but sell TIC (tenants in common) interests in shopping centers, apartment buildings, and so on.

Commercial and Industrial Properties

Industrial buildings are not easy investments. Most industrial properties are built for one specific use, and changes in the economy can affect these properties greatly, especially if they cater to small business manufacturing operations. In contrast to residential properties (everyone needs a place to live), the pool of prospective tenants for industrial buildings is much smaller. This is especially true during a recessionary period when landlords are forced to lower rental rates to fill vacancies. A situation like this could result in a negative cash flow for years, and could even lead to bankruptcy.

Conversion Properties

These have become real money makers for investors. Though they require a lot more work, there are plenty of advantages. In a conversion situation, you change a unit from a tenant rental to occupant ownership. This way, the tenant, who becomes an owner, develops a vested interest in the property. Fees are split for landscaping, maintenance, and other common areas. To evaluate this option as an investor:

- Know the zoning in the area.
- In new buildings, check for risks such as radon, soil problems, mold, termites, etc.
- In older buildings, check for lead paint and other hazardous substances.
- Hire an environmental engineer to give you a complete report.

If you live in a university town, converting apartments to student rentals can be very lucrative. For example, if a two-bedroom apartment was renting for $450, buyers of student rentals can market their properties at $300 per room.

The advantages of conversion properties are threefold: (1) They bring higher rates of return, (2) the prospect of flipping for hefty profits, (3) and they usually require limited cash. Often, most of the project can be financed, including the conversion costs. However, lenders prefer to work with experienced investors in conversions.

Conversion Ownership

Recently, I've noticed a trend of commercial rental buildings being converted into condos and resold to individuals. I talked with an owner who, with his partners, was pursuing this project.

His building was located in the heart of town where professionals would want to be located. The units were renting for $15 to $17 per square foot. Once converted, the partners priced them from $140,000 to $200,000, plus a monthly maintenance fee of $150.

Most of their units went quickly. Even as our market slowed, I noticed more of these condo units being built. If a professional needs office space, would he or she be better off renting or owning? "At least they would have something to resell," said the owner of the converted complex.

Turnover is very low. The professionals who buy into this concept seem to be able to afford it. Overall, not having your rent raised seems a big selling point.

Look into conversions in your area. Learn the zoning for apartments that are turned into condos to see if this is a feasible and marketable idea. Once again, do your due diligence before you begin to tackle this type of project.

A Final Word on Selecting Properties

Smart investing requires you to do your homework and keep abreast of market trends. Keep a close eye on the economy, and try to keep a step ahead by determining how market trends will affect the neighborhoods where you own property.

A good example of this is in Fort Collins, Colorado. Hewlett-Packard, a major employer, has recently laid off large numbers of people locally, as have other high-tech companies. That's important to know, but it has had almost no effect on the housing market. That's because Fort Collins, in a recent survey that tracks repeat sales of homes, ranked number three in the nation for housing appreciation. The net effect this has had on my investing is that I am now considering making a

Don't Forget

Know the demographics of your own investment market. Are more people moving into your area than out of it? If so, housing shortages develop. Check real estate activity with your local Board of Realtors to determine if you are in a buyer's or seller's market. The number of foreclosures will also give you insight into your market trends.

30-minute drive north to Cheyenne, Wyoming, to check out the market there. Prices will be lower, and as Fort Collins becomes ever more expensive, more and more people will need to find cheaper housing within commuting distance.

It's a Wrap

✓ Do your homework!

✓ Careful planning will help you avoid costly mistakes.

✓ Single family homes can help spread your risk.

✓ When buying condos and town houses, know the homeowner associations' bylaws first.

✓ Duplexes are an excellent start.

✓ Multiunit buildings offer greater profitability.

✓ Know the demographics of your investment market.

CHAPTER 3

Flipping Properties

→ I want to show a profit in a short period of time.

→ Do I know what an option is?

→ Do I know what an assignment is?

→ Do I understand the risks of flipping?

Property Flipping

A "flip" involves buying a property below market value and then "flipping" it to another buyer at a profit. This tactic carries some risks, but if you become skilled at it, you can reap great profits on your investments in a short period of time.

Note that you can only flip a property that was bought below market value. You must lock in the price with the seller, but not take title to the property. The costs of that transaction will eat up your profits if your aim is to do a quick turnaround for resale. It's best to have a buyer waiting in the wings or have a plan on where to find one. Lastly, provide full disclosure. Make sure all parties involved are aware of what you are doing. You are providing a sale for a seller who wants out and a home for a buyer who wants in. Why shouldn't you get a profit for bringing the two of them together?

The best way to lock in a purchase price without buying a property is to take an option on it or an assignment. An option gives you the opportunity to buy at a set price at some future date. With an option, the benefit to the seller is that he or she has a legal commitment of purchase at a set price. If you present an option offer to a seller and the seller accepts, you then are obliged to put up option money, which locks you into a fixed price and a specific date for closing the deal. You in turn "exercise the option" by either closing on the property as specified or selling the option itself to another buyer at a profit.

The advantages of an option are that you have fixed the price—it cannot increase. There is no qualifying, and you do not have to obtain a mortgage. Also, the option money is somewhat less than what is expected for a down payment.

Get Started

How to Flip a Property

1. Locate a property below market value.

2. Present your offer to the seller.

3. Once the seller accepts, lock in the price and agree on a reasonable time interval before closing to allow you to resell the property.

4. Find a new buyer who actually purchases the property from the seller.

5. They close, and you receive the difference in profit.

Upside-Down Deals Ruin a Career

Many investors make money on flipping deals. Honest people like Steve make a living buying undervalued properties and then selling them with clean appraisals for a fair market price. His marketing campaign to attract buyers is one of the best I have ever seen. He kept a database of buyers who looked at other properties he owned. When they did not get a particular property, he asked if they would like to be on his mailing list for other properties.

Each time Steve found another property and had it under contract, he would market it by simply mailing out a color postcard of the house with a description to his database of prospects. At last count he had over 500 people on his mailing list.

But sometimes things go sour. A competitor of Steve's was not as ethical. He would inflate the sale price of the properties he had under contract. The properties weren't worth what this competitor sold them for. He obtained MAI (made as instructed) appraisals for buyers to take to the bank. The bank made loans to the buyers based on these inflated appraised values. Steve's competitor got large profits off his deals, but when the buyers defaulted and properties went into foreclosure, the bank realized they were stuck with an upside-down situation.

The only person coming out ahead was the flipper. This happened so frequently in Steve's area that the major banking institutions, and even finance companies, now refuse to allow loans on "flipped" property. This has just about put Steve out of business.

Because you don't own the property, you are not responsible for mortgage payments, taxes, insurance, and maintenance or repairs that come up during the agreed-upon interval before closing.

The drawbacks to options are that you do have to put up money, and if the deal falls through, you've lost it. Also, if you don't exercise your option before it expires, you lose the option money. If property values go down during the option period, you will have a harder time finding a willing buyer.

Another popular way to flip properties is with assignment of purchase. When you present your purchase offer, after your name include the words "and/or assigns." This means that you yourself will buy the property or whomever you assign the contract to. Assignments of purchase close more quickly than options, and little actual cash is involved. You put up the deposit and are reimbursed by the person you assigned the contract to. An assignment does, however, oblige you to close the deal, so make sure you write in escape clauses as a way out if circumstances change. Here are some examples of escape clauses that you can specify in your purchase offer:

- Finance contingency: The offer is contingent on you obtaining financing at the interest rate and number of years that you require.

- Disclosure contingency: You must approve all seller's disclosures with regard to the property.

- Professional inspection: You must approve the inspector's report, usually within a short period of time after you and the seller have signed the contract.

Over the past few years, buyers who purchase properties at market and then inflate the property to the new buyer have given flipping a bad name. In these cases, the investor procures an unrealistically high appraisal. The lender, based on this appraisal, makes a larger loan than is justified. The buyer—usually someone who doesn't understand market value—gets in over his head and loses out. The bank is stuck with a bad loan that was made on bad market information. If either Fannie Mae or Freddie Mac is involved, the investor can be sued both in civil and criminal court.

Don't Forget

Many investors take their profit in the form of paper. This allows them to create the deal they want. Be sure you have a clause in the contract with the new buyer that states this contract cannot be assumed by anyone else.

Rules for Making Money on Investment Properties

- Buy single or small multifamily housing.
- Look in better, but not the best, neighborhoods.
- Look for strong tenants' markets.
- Buy only when the property has a good price/rent ratio.
- Know what your rental expenses will be.
- Go for favorable terms.
- Get a bargain price, not an inflated value.
- Remember: The sale price is just the seller's first offer.
- Never buy far from home if possible. "Acres of diamonds in your own backyard."

There are specific sources for finding below-market properties suitable for quick flips, which we will discuss in detail in the section on finding properties. Briefly, though, these are through auctions, contractors, real estate brokers, lenders, and other professionals involved with real estate, such as attorneys and appraisers.

Note: In many states flipping properties can be a problem. Many lenders will not get involved with flipped properties. They want the investor to own the property for a period of time before they resell. Therefore, this flipping strategy should be taken with caution. You may want to check with local lenders and legal counsel in your area before you pursue this strategy.

Don't Forget

Flipping properties carries certain risks. For example, you may not be able to turn property as quickly as you'd planned. Be aware that "fast" is a relative term in real estate. A fast transaction where financing is needed can take from 45 to 60 days. Be realistic in your expectations on how quickly you can turn a property. If you can't find a buyer for your project when you are ready to flip, consider converting it to a rental or a lease option. Don't fall into the trap of overspending on fix-up expenses and not being able to make a profit on resale. Always do a property analysis, and know the hard costs before you buy. We'll say more about this in the rehabbing section.

It's a Wrap

✓ Flipping can reap profits in a short period of time.

✓ Options lock in purchase prices.

✓ Assignments mean you or someone else buys the property.

✓ Flipping carries risks, and it's important to understand them.

✓ Don't overspend—know the hard costs before you buy.

CHAPTER 4

Different Purchasing Choices Explained

Do I Need to Read This Chapter?

➡ You want to understand the different ways to go about purchasing.

➡ You don't know what a lease option is.

➡ What advantages are there in rehab properties?

➡ You've heard of foreclosure sales, but don't know how to pursue them.

➡ You've never heard of tax lien certificates.

➡ You don't know how zoning laws can affect you.

Purchasing Property

Lease Options

Lower risk, higher rents, and guaranteed profits are the main reasons to enter into lease options. Here are the main points in favor of such agreements:

- You retain title to the property until the tenant exercises his or her option. This means you avoid the "due on sale" issue. A due-on-sale clause in a mortgage entitles the lender to demand full payment of all money due on your loan when you sell or transfer title to the property.

- Because the lease governs the landlord-tenant relationship, getting a nonpaying renter out of a property is accomplished through an eviction, which is easier than if your method of selling was a land contract or deed of trust.

- Because the lease and the option are associated in the minds of your tenants, they start thinking and acting like homeowners instead of renters. You can put language in your lease option that makes the tenants responsible for all repairs, thereby cutting down on your fix-up and maintenance costs.

- Instead of collecting a refundable security deposit when your tenants move in, you collect a nonrefundable option fee. This is often much more than a security deposit.

- The option clause also allows you to charge higher rents by building in rent credits—actually purchase price credits that contribute toward a buyer's down payment requirements. This obviously increases your monthly cash flow from the property, and rent credits are nonrefundable. The more credit you extend to the tenant, the more committed the tenant becomes to completing the sale.

- You can structure the option so that when it expires, the tenant-buyer can renew it with another cash payment. This keeps them invested in the property.

For investors wanting to buy property this way, options lock in a purchase price and terms for a fixed interval of time. If you decide you want the property, you exercise your option. If not, you only lose the price you paid for the option. Overall, this is a great way to control property with minimal risk.

Finding Lease Option Opportunities

Property managers and real estate agents can often direct you to these sellers. Also check newspaper classifieds. Sometimes they will specifically advertise availability of a lease option. You can also place your own ad. For example, in the "Homes for Sale" section, you could place an ad such as this:

Need a 3 bedroom/2 bath home in the southeast part of town. Would like an option to buy. Can afford $1,000 per month. Call (*your name*) at (*your number*).

Protecting My Contract

When I moved to Colorado in the early 1990s, I did not want to buy a property immediately. Nor did I want to throw my money away on rent.

I found a property in a very nice neighborhood that was convenient to shopping and the interstate. The owners were selling the property on their own and wanted $118,000, well above the median price that year for property.

I sat down with the sellers over breakfast and negotiated a fair deal between us. We ended up with a lease option to buy the property within 18 months for $105,000. My option deposit was $2,500. The rent was $750 per month, with no rent credits. They accepted our offer, and I signed a contract prepared by a local attorney. Then I flew home to pack and move.

A week later the sellers contacted me, asking to be released from the contract. They had found another buyer for the home, who was willing to pay them $115,000 cash. They offered $5,000 and a return of our option deposit if I would cancel the contract. I refused.

I moved in, leased the property for six months, then exercised the option. Three years later I moved, but kept the property as a rental. Last year I sold the property for close to double what I paid for it. Lease options are a great way to tie up property with minimal risk.

Quick Tips

For sellers, a lease option agreement offers some of the benefits of a seller-financed sale while avoiding many of its pitfalls.

Are you handy with a hammer or a paintbrush? Don't overestimate your abilities in this area. Your time is not free. If you can spend it more wisely on other activities, hire the work out. By the same token, be realistic about working with contractors. They don't always show up on time, and sometimes their work is substandard. Inflating fees is not uncommon. Here are a few ways to prepare yourself for working with contractors:

- In most large bookstores and online, you can find construction estimator guides that estimate the time needed for various types of work.

- Get bids on rehabbing the property from at least three contractors. Check references, licenses, and insurance before hiring anyone.

Striking Gold

On Sundays, I like to drive the streets to have a look at what's for sale. Recently, I came across an open house sign outside a very expensive property. This 6,200 square foot executive home was priced at $799,000. I knew that the property had been sitting on the market for four months.

Chatting with the realtor, I learned that the owner really wanted to sell. His newest wife wanted a different home, so he built another $799,000 home and was saddled with two jumbo loans. The realtor said the owner would consider a lease option. So, we discussed this offer:

Sale Price: $750,000

Option consideration: $2,000

Rent $2,000 per month for a year

I knew the property could easily be rented for $2,500 per month and possibly $3,000. If I rented it to an executive for $2,750 per month, I could pocket $750 per month for 11 months (taking into account my $2,000 option consideration), or $30,250 for the term of the lease. I could sell the option to the tenant for only $20,000. If the property jumped in value to $850,000, the tenant would be able to buy this property for $750,000 plus my $20,000 option, so the cost to the tenant would be $770,000.

The owner would have his mortgage payment made and a better chance to sell the property, and would keep my $2,000 if I didn't exercise the option or find someone who would. The tenant would get a beautiful home and a year to come up with the cash for real estate. I make $50,250 by the end of the year. Now that's a win-win deal!

Quick Tips

Lease options do not work everywhere. Check the law in your state to see if there have been recent changes to lease/options.

- You can contract with consultants who specialize in assisting investors with rehabbing property, although they will charge a percentage of the finished job, including labor and materials. They can, however, act as a general contractor for you.

Get Started

Rehab Properties

Are you able to visualize an attractive residence when looking at a run-down property? If so, you should consider rehabbing properties. Buying "handyman specials" to fix up and sell at a profit is a great way investors can make money in real estate, if their personality is suited to the project.

Rehabbing requires careful planning before you buy. You won't make any money if you end up paying more on repairs than the property can justify for a profitable resale amount. Educate yourself thoroughly beforehand as to which repairs are easily handled and which ones signal problem areas to avoid.

Watch for high-cost items such as cracked foundations, lead paint in older buildings, soil instability, or drainage problems. If you don't know how to evaluate these things, find an expert. Basing your decision to buy on a "guess" as to what the cost of renovations will be will almost certainly end up costing you money! Always make your purchase offer contingent upon approving a professional inspection. This allows you to back out of the deal or negotiate for a lower price if the inspection report is worse than you anticipated. The cost of the inspection is well worth your peace of mind.

Concentrate on improving the areas of the property that are most lived in or most readily seen. New carpet, fresh paint, and fixing up the front entry, bathrooms, and kitchen will add the most value to a rehab. Use landscaping to eliminate negative views. Create more usable space, such as installing closet organizers to increase storage in smaller closets.

Don't Forget

As a general rule, limit your improvements to cosmetic items. Things such as worn carpet, broken windows, broken sinks or toilets, leaking tubs or showers, or dead landscaping can be improved on a budget.

Make sure your bids are priced by the job, not by an hourly fee. Cost overruns can ruin a project.

If you're considering going into the rehab business and want to tackle major renovations, a trusted crew is a must. Make sure the contractors you hire are licensed and bonded. Check references and get time commitments for completing the job in writing. Add a clause stating you can deduct a percentage of the bid price if the job is not completed on time. Other tips:

Rehab Heaven in Memphis

My friend is a hard money lender. He works with a rehabber whom he charges 5 points and 12 percent interest per month with a renewable three months at another 5 points. Let's look at how this works for both parties.

The rehabber finds a property for $40,000. My friend lends him the money, less 5 points. The rehabber walks away with a little under $38,000. He pays for all costs and fees associated with the loan. He has a full-time crew that rehabs the property. He then turns around and resells the property for $65,000 on an FHA loan, which was appraised at $65,000 by FHA to first-time home buyers.

Last year the rehabber did 57 loans with my friend. He has done over 200 rehabs since 2001. All were done the same way for around the same price and the same type of short-term loan.

What did my friend get? He made $2,000 plus 12 percent interest for the period of time the money was borrowed. They do a real closing, and the hard money lender is secured by a note and deed of trust on the property. My friend makes a great return, and the rehabber is making a good profit on each deal! Now that's good business.

Lately, more investors are using their retirement dollars to make loans. They get the profit and fees back into their IRA or 401(k) tax deferred or tax free, depending on the type of plan they have!

- Price the job by the project, not by the hour.
- Specify that the cost of any repairs for damage incurred while working will be deducted from the final payment.
- In many cases, a city building inspector may be involved to make sure your project is in line with code. Include all your projects under one building permit. Each inspection entails a fee.

Note: You can hire consultants to get the job done, but they charge a flat fee plus a percentage of the cost of the work at completion. Not exactly the way to make money if you're a real estate investor.

Rehabbing News

There has been talk of a lobby being started that will help rehabbers and investors who buy properties wholesale deal with government issues.

Due to the longer seasoning requirements, these types of investors have to sit on property longer, which cuts into their profit potential.

A Cautionary Tale

My friends wanted to rehab their offices and make the area a more pleasant one for their clients. They hired a contractor to find the crew and rehab the property. They were promised a finished job within 60 days.

Everything went wrong! The crew failed to show up half the time, the contractor was working on other projects and made my friends a low priority, since this was a commercial job and he assumed they would not mind if it was a little delayed. Wrong! My friends went crazy. The husband finally starting ripping out the walls himself. The office was a dust bowl where one could barely breathe for weeks. Eventually, after my friends threatened a lawsuit, the contractor hired another crew to finish the job.

Though the improvement looks great, my friends will never go through this again. Rehab? They are only buying new!

The government feels that there are some "bad-apple investors" who don't really rehab property, but instead inflate prices and commit fraud. This, along with lenders being upside down on properties that have loans in excess of fair market value, has forced intervention.

Of course, the rehabber and wholesaler are affected. To learn more about this potential lobby that is in its infancy stage, e-mail the National Real Estate Investors Association (www.NREIA.org). They will provide you with the contact information of the lobbyist in Washington, D.C., who is actively involved in regulatory issues.

Foreclosures

When a property owner defaults on his loan, the lender can foreclose and take over the property. After a legally determined period of time, the lender "sells" the property to the highest bidder "on the courthouse steps." Typically, the lender (a bank or other institution) is the highest bidder and takes control of the property to try to sell it. This is called an REO (real estate owned) property of the institution.

You can acquire a foreclosed property by buying the property from the homeowner before the foreclosed auction, by being the highest bidder at the auction, or by buying the property from the bank or institution that took it over as an REO. Let's look at each of these methods.

Buy from the Owner before the Auction

An owner facing foreclosures is obviously an individual in dire straits facing loss of credit and the public disgrace of losing his home due to financial failure on his part. These people are always depressed and often angry. This is not a happy situation to walk into, but sometimes a losing proposition can be turned around.

I like to approach these people initially by sending them a postcard that says, "I pay cash for your real estate equity. Facing foreclosure? Call now for a free, no-obligation consultation on how to save your credit. Call Lisa at 123–4567." Soon after, I call them and say something like, "I'm an investor looking for property in your area. I've heard you've been having some problems, and I wondered if we could work out a win-win solution together. I buy your property, and you save your credit." Then the negotiation process begins.

Righting a foreclosure can be expensive: Foreclosed properties are often in poor condition for a variety of reasons. (An owner facing foreclosure often takes his anger out on the property: "If I can't keep it, I'm going to make sure no one else wants it!") So you have to weigh the costs of making the property presentable again. Also, you will have to make up the back payments, and so on. There will be penalties associated with the loan default and other assorted fees. If you need a new loan, that too will include points, fees, and title insurance. Figure that these will amount to about 5 percent of the loan amount.

Quick Tips

Getting clear title to foreclosure property is not always easy. Buy title insurance as additional protection. Some states have laws protecting individual owners from being preyed upon by fortune-hunting investors. (Typically, the investor will buy a foreclosure for much less than the original purchase price.) Such laws allow for a period of time for rescission of a sales agreement when an owner is in default on his loan. This means if they can cure the loan, or make up the back payments and get current within the rescission period, they get to stay in their home and the investor loses the deal.

The period of time varies by state. Make sure you have access to a good real estate attorney who is familiar with all the rules pertaining in your state.

Be the Highest Bidder

When you use the second method of "buying at the courthouse steps," your offer must be in cash. You have to have your financing in place beforehand. The risk is that you receive no title or other guarantees as to the status of the property. You may think you're bidding on a first mortgage and then find out that you are in third position!

Buy from the Bank

The third method is buying REOs. Lenders are not interested in being property managers, so they will usually wait three to six months before initiating foreclosure proceedings on a property. They do this hoping the owner will right the loan, because banks cannot pay their depositors with real estate. Once a property is back with a bank, however, they employ a real estate company to resell the property for them.

 Find the company and agents who handle foreclosures for the lender in question. The lender will be paying those agents commissions for finding you. If a property you're interested in is under contract already, make a backup offer. Many investors can't get the financing in place quickly enough, so you need to be standing next in line. Offer a higher price if the lender is willing to finance you. Some lenders will even include a fix-up allowance in the loan. The lender should pay all normal closing costs. Try sending a letter to the bank letting them know that you are an investor who buys REOs.

Don't Forget

The chief drawbacks to buying an REO is that they are often sold "as is" with no disclosures. This can result in some nasty surprises. Also, always be sure the property is vacant when you buy it. Evicting the previous owner can cost you thousands! Never rent or resell to the person who lived in the house previously. Again, buy title insurance.

Buy a Lien Position

Another way to prepare a foreclosure is to buy a junior lien position to the property before it hits the courthouse steps and wipes out their investments. When working with lien holders, keep in mind that generally the lower the position of the lien holder, the greater the discount they are willing to accept.

Short Sales

I was recently on a cruise as the marketing advisor for the National Real Estate Investors Association. The week-long cruise was a continuing education at sea for real estate investors. (For more information on the cruise or on a local REIA near you, visit the NREIA.org Web site.)

On the cruise, the buzz words were "short sales." In fact, one speaker talked about short selling a note/private seller-financed mortgage, and two other speakers also used this strategy as part of their presentations.

What was amazing to me were the words "short sales." After hearing one presentation, I thought: These speakers are talking about negotiating with a bank when a person is in default of his loan. By negotiating at this point, the bank may sell the property at a discount so it does not have to incur the costs of foreclosure and eventual resale and can get the property off its books.

What it came down to was: buying paper and property from the bank at a discount. Having the distressed seller involved, with the correct documentation in place, so the bank knows the borrower is walking from the property.

I have no problem with this strategy. It has been around for years. It was just never termed a "short sale." Why mention this? Because the strategies from years ago are the same strategies today. In my opinion, there is no "get rich quick" to real estate. It is developing your strategy and continually moving forward and doing deals.

There are many spins on how one does things, but from a terminology perspective, not much has changed. Banks have been "short selling" (discounting property) to get it off their books for years.

Bargains in Government Repo

HUD

Check whether there are HUD homes in your area. On the Internet, log onto www.hud.gov/index.html. There will be a referral agent's name for your region. You can contact that agent and go see the property you're interested in. The maximum loan amount with HUD can change yearly. Get in touch with HUD to find out this maximum.

Most homes will fall into the moderate price range. Make sure you know the fair market value of the area where the property is located. The government will require 10 percent down from investors, nothing down from owner-occupants; the latter are given preference over investors. Although they say they may reopen their FHA $277,000 program (acquisition and rehab) to investors, they have not done so as of this writing.

Check with HUD directly if you have questions about financing. Properties are sold "as is" with one exception: They do require a lead paint disclosure to the buyer. Make sure you always include the contingency of inspection approval in your purchase offer.

For a HUD contract package checklist, visit www.HUD.gov.

VA Repos

Like HUD, you must go through a local real estate agent who represents the VA's property management program. Typically, these agents advertise locally in newspapers. Check www.homeloans.va.gov/rlcweb.htm to see if there are properties for sale in your area. The VA will finance you, but you'll get a better deal with a cash offer. The VA also has an extensive regional rehab program so that they can get higher prices. Again, get a professional inspection before your offer is accepted.

Fannie Mae Properties

Fannie Mae is one of the main secondary lenders. It underwrites all types of single family homes, including detached properties, condos, and town homes. Properties are listed with an agent and also appear in the Multiple Listing Service. Any agent in the local board can show you a home and make an offer on your behalf. The listing agent presents this to Fannie Mae for approval.

Quick Tips

You can find a list of homes available through Fannie Mae at www.fanniemae.com/homes.html.

Make an offer on a home that looks promising. Unlike HUD or VA, with Fannie Mae properties you can write contingencies into the contract. You must be preapproved by a lender to have your offer accepted. Homes are sold "as is." Fannie Mae does offer its own REO financing, but it's really no better than you can do elsewhere.

Freddie Mac also offers single family houses, condos, and town houses, but their bargains are not as good. Their homes are offered through a select group of lenders. Their Web site is www.homesteps.com.

Other Government Repo Web Sites

Customs: www.treas.gov/auctions/customs

Veteran Affairs: www.homeloans.va.gov/homes/html/

FDIC: www.fdic.gov/buying/owned/index.html

GSA: http://propertydisposal.gsa.gov.property/

IRS: www.treas.gov/auctions/irs/

SBA: http://appl.sba.gov/pfsales/dsp_search.html

U.S. Marshal: www.usdoj.gov/marshals/assets/nsl.html/

Don't Forget

A note on IRS sales: Some foreclosure buyers prefer IRS sales over foreclosure sales, because generally there are fewer bidders. This is because IRS sales are not as well publicized as foreclosure sales. Usually, it is just one publication and posting on the property.

IRS tax liens are general liens against the property. They do not have the priority of property tax liens. Therefore, when a property is sold by the IRS for unpaid income taxes, the purchaser takes the property subject to all liens, so a careful title check is a must before you buy. Realize that taxpayers have a period of 180 days to redeem their property after an IRS sale.

Tax Lien Certificates

Did you know that you could invest in delinquent property taxes? In almost all cases, unpaid property taxes take the first lien position on the title of a property, no matter how encumbered the property is. This means that delinquent property taxes can never be wiped away by the foreclosure of any lien, including the IRS and state tax liens. The property tax must be paid before clear title to a property can pass from one owner to the next.

When delinquent taxes are sold to an investor, you are in first position. Should the specified time elapse and the payments are not yet made to clear the title, you, the investor, can sue for deed to the property.

Counties need revenue from property taxes to fund government operations, such as schools, police, and fire departments. They cannot afford any loss of revenue. When the period of time in which a homeowner must have paid taxes elapses, the county has the right to sell a tax lien certificate or a tax deed (depending on the state) at an auction.

Quick Tips

Many states have gone so far as to use marketing tools to raise awareness of the money to be made at tax sales. For example, they might raise the return on investors' money or shorten the length of the redemption period. In most areas around the country, local governments handle these sales. In Texas, they are farmed out to attorneys.

Tax Lien Certificates, Wyoming Style

Wyoming is a good state to invest in tax liens. They pay a higher interest rate than some. There is not a lot of competition, as in, say, Florida.

My first experience with tax liens was in 1992 when a friend and I researched Natrona County, Wyoming. I had been told this was tax lien heaven. The county had been advertising the tax sales with the property addresses in the legal section of the newspaper for the last six weeks before the auction.

I was investing in the certificates with my IRA. I instructed my administrators to make checks payable to the Natrona County Treasurer, and I took these to the sale.

What an experience! I worked with a third party who lived in the area and knew which properties were worth buying the certificates on, meaning we would eventually get paid off. We were each issued a number, and just like lotto, the ping pong ball would spin around and if your number came up, you could either buy the certificate or pass. I looked to our local expert for advice.

I was able to purchase a half-dozen or so certificates. The rest of the checks went back to my administrators. I received 18 percent interest for the first year, then 15 percent each year for the next three years. I have to renew the certificate every year to stay in first position. If the homeowner still has not paid off his or her taxes in year four, I could sue for the tax deed. This has never happened to me. The last certificate of the batch was paid off in year three.

I also went to Cheyenne to try to invest in tax certificates. Cheyenne is much closer to where I live, and I could view these properties on my own. However, there were so few certificates for sale that I didn't pursue this further. Same state, different counties, very different results!

Tax Deeds vs. Tax Lien Certificates

If your state is a tax deed state, you purchase the actual deed to the property at the tax sale. If a redemption period is specified, once it's over, the property is yours. If your state sells tax lien certificates, it sells you a first-position lien on the property, which means that, following any redemption period, you must then foreclose on the homeowner to take title to the property.

Get Started

Your first order of business is to learn whether your state is a tax deed or a tax lien state. After that, educate yourself about your state's procedures:

• Visit the tax assessor or delinquent tax department and ask how they publish their notices for auction and how often they hold tax sales.

• View the property you are interested in before the sale takes place. Most counties advertise for four to six weeks in advance of the sale.

• Try to get inside the property if possible.

• Know the fair market value of the property itself, as well as surrounding properties.

• Make sure you understand the bidding process for tax sales before committing money.

It's a good idea to learn by observing first.

Buying to Hold

Millions of people have made money in real estate by investing long-term in property to rent for cash flow. There will always be tenants to assist you in paying off your loan with their monthly rent. Your upside is cash flow and equity gain. Of course, you have to buy right initially. One of the laws of real estate investing is that you make money when you buy, not when you sell. You also must structure your financing so you can make your payments from the rent generated by your property. Thus, only buy property when prices are reasonable and a rental break-even is possible. Here's a summary of the best advice for a buy-to-hold strategy:

Dos and Don'ts When Buying Real Estate

• Do put all terms and conditions of sale in writing.
• Do record your deed immediately.
• Do check property for easements or encroachments.
• Do insist on a property inspection clause in the contract offer.

Watch Out—You Never Know What Can Happen with Zoning!

I purchased a property in 1994 in a family neighborhood of nice single family homes. The neighborhood was surrounded by vacant land on three sides. Before we signed, I asked what was going to be built here. I was assured that the land was all zoned for single family residential dwellings.

Two years later a builder of major apartment complexes bought one tract. He put up over 300 units. Yes, they are nice, but I would not consider this residential housing. A year later town homes and patio homes went up on another tract. Yes, this is residential housing, but I was starting to feel that someone had lied to me.

Finally, the last tract was sold and rezoned as commercial. An office building and large parking lot were built. The neighborhood appealed to the city not to do this but lost, because the owner of the office building was connected with the original builder/developer who would be constructing the building for commercial use. These were powerful people. We were just the little guys. We lost.

Today, the area is a mixed community of nice properties, apartments, and commercial. But that was not what I was told. The moral: If you are buying in an area not fully developed, ask lots of questions, but don't assume you'll be given the straight scoop. The other moral: City governments favor big money! What a surprise!

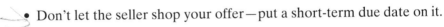

- Don't let the seller shop your offer—put a short-term due date on it.
- Don't give the seller your deposit. Make the check out to an escrow company or directly to the bank.
- Don't sign a contract without legal advice.
- Don't get caught in a rezoning problem.

It's a Wrap

✓ There are many ways to purchase property—choose what works for you.

✓ Lease options can offer lower risk, higher rents, and guaranteed profits.

✓ When considering rehab properties, don't overestimate your handyman capabilities.

✔ Foreclosures are often sold "as is," so they may include some unpleasant structural surprises.

✔ Familiarize yourself with your state's property tax laws and procedures.

✔ Only buy when prices are reasonable and a rental break-even is possible.

CHAPTER 5

How to Find the Right Property

Do I Need to Read This Chapter?

→ You're ready to start looking for a property to purchase.

→ You don't know if you should work with a realtor.

→ You don't know what relocation companies are or how they can help you.

→ You want to learn how marketing will help you find property to purchase.

→ You don't know which marketing methods will work for you.

Finding Property

There are many, many ways to find property deals. These range from the conventional to the creative. One of the easiest ways is using the Internet from the comfort of your home office.

Realty Web sites offer good, detailed property descriptions, usually with pictures, and sometimes even with virtual tours. Locator maps, e-mail addresses, and phone numbers of sellers or agents make preliminary checking of properties quick and efficient. However, there is no substitute for on-site property viewing. The Internet is also a great research tool for gathering data and statistics on neighborhoods, title reports, and foreclosures.

Quick Tips

Here are some helpful Web sites to check out:

- www.dataquick.com

- www.realtor.com (for agent listings)

- www.owners.com

- www.homebytes.com

- www.ehomes.com

Mold: Be Aware

If you purchased a property recently, you were probably required to sign an addendum concerning mold. Many real estate investors are concerned with this issue. Before you close on a property, do your due diligence.

Don't Forget

Mold must be disclosed. Make sure you do your due diligence before you buy the property. If you sign off without some inspection, you are taking a risk, although some investors feel that an inspection is not necessary.

Mold is very expensive to remediate. The only way to get rid of mold is with a commercial-strength bleach solution. Though that would not seem like a big deal, it can sometimes cost the investor the price of his or her property.

As one example, I was reading over a commercial lease agreement in which the landlord had a clause that basically said that if any mold is found after we occupy the premises, the responsibility of remediation—getting rid of the mold—would be ours, the tenant. Everyone who read the lease felt the responsibility would be the landlord's, not the tenant's. We refused to sign this lease.

Here's another example:

Boy George

George was a beginning investor. He attended his local real estate investor club and a few conventions and seminars on investing in real estate. He purchased everyone's courses. After spending thousands of dollars on course materials, George decided his niche would be as a rehabber.

He bought a 3,700 square foot commercial building in an area of the country that experiences humidity. The building was over 50 years old and needed some major rehabbing. George figured he would double his money when the rehabbing was completed and he resold the property within six months.

George hired the work out. The rehab was 25 percent over his expected budget. He dipped into savings to pay for the work. He put the property on the market.

It took longer than expected for it to sell. George depleted his entire savings while this property sat idle. He finally got a contract, subject to inspections. The buyers did a mold inspection and, sure enough, the building was loaded with mold.

It cost George almost as much as his initial investment to remediate the property. Worse, since he was out of savings, he had no choice but to go into his retirement funds. Pretty expensive seminar, wasn't it?

Ways to Find Property

Classified Ads

Look for words indicating motivation to sell: "Relocating" or "Must Sell." Or place your own ad. Motivated sellers will read your ad and call you. Following are some examples I've used.

Sell me your home...

FAST for cash! Quick Closes — As Is

Call Lisa 123–4567

I pay cash for your real estate equity,

even if you are delinquent or in foreclosure.

Call for a no-cost consultation: 123–4567

Farming

One way I find property is to "farm" for it. I have four distinct areas that I monitor on a frequent basis, like a farmer tends his fields. I know every property that has sold in the last year, and what the asking price was versus what it sold for.

At times I have used paper door hangers with my name and phone number on them that affixes to a doorknob. I leave it on the doors of homes in my farm area. I ask that the homeowner call me before they list the property for sale. They could save thousands in real estate commissions! This little system has worked well for me over the years.

I also do drive-bys, go to open houses, and call property managers to ask if they know of any homes that a landlord may be listing for sale in these particular neighborhoods. I tell them I would appreciate a contact should a landlord decide to sell. I may be able to arrange for the property manager to keep managing the home for a period of time if I can get the right deal. If a property manager knows he can keep the business, he is usually willing to become a referral source.

My personal strategy is to farm areas that are not in starter neighborhoods. They would be considered step-up areas. Starter neighborhoods are great investments, though. Because they cost less, you can cash-flow the property and receive more income. I notice, however, more of a turnover in the starters that I have left in my portfolio. I think this is because the homes are smaller and older. People outgrow them and want larger, newer homes. There is nothing wrong with the neighborhoods themselves; the properties just create more management than I care to have.

When you become familiar with the neighborhood you wish to buy in, you will often get advance notice of anything coming on the market. Over the last two months I have personally looked at three different properties before they were listed in the MLS. Two I found by simply walking around in the neighborhood, and one was from a realtor working with the seller on the home they are buying.

Get Started

How do you begin farming the areas where you want to seek investment property?

- Know what you are willing to spend. Don't waste time in neighborhoods where the market price is double what you're looking for.

- Get a good feel for the neighborhood. Can the children walk to school? Is a grocery store nearby? These things are important if you are renting to families.

- If you are buying rentals in a university area, put a flyer up at the student union. If you are rehabbing an area that has growing potential, focus on the storefronts and other businesses in that area. Ask if you can leave a flyer stating that you are looking for a property to fix up.

Vacant Property/Out-of-Town Owners

Ask the neighbors of these properties if they know where the owner can be located. If they don't know, go to the county property tax assessor's office. There you can learn where and to whom the property tax statements are mailed.

"For Sale by Owner" Sign

These individuals don't want to pay real estate commissions. You negotiate with them directly for properties. You can find FSBO listings on the Internet as well as by doing drive-bys and looking at local publications that are devoted to FSBO properties. Also, attorneys who advertise in these publications are an excellent source of referrals, especially if they get to do the closing documents.

Builders

As an incentive for buyers, many homebuilders offer low down payments and attractive financing. For example, Ryan Homes recently offered rates of 4.99 percent in the first year, 5.99 percent the second year, and 6.5 percent for the next 28 years. Read the builder ads in your local newspaper and contact them directly. Also, try to negotiate your deal with landscaping included.

Retirees

Often, these homeowners are considering downsizing. They are in a good position to assist with financing, because they like collecting monthly income to supplement their retirement income.

Builders

In 1994, I bought a 2,500-square-foot house that the builder had built as a spec. His asking price was $220,000. We ran comps and knew that the price was fair. So, in order to tie up the property, we offered him full price if he would upgrade the appliances, landscape both the front and back yard, install fencing, add two garage door openers to the three-car garage, put tile in the bathrooms where they had carpeted, and add central air.

Now we had over $25,000 worth of upgrades, did not have to deal with landscaping, and a year later turned around and sold the house for $290,000. The builder got out from under his high interest construction loan, and though he did not make any money on this deal, had one less house in his inventory.

Another builder built two dozen homes in a high-end neighborhood. He found a more desirable location and started building higher-end homes there. These beauties cost him well over $300,000.

His staff sold only five homes in a year, so he became desperate to get out. One of the homes had a lovely floor plan; the asking price was $454,000. I asked what he had in it, but he refused to say, so I offered $375,000 just to see what would happen. He countered! He said I could have the property for $415,000. I thought this was still too much.

As I started to walk away, the builder said, "Okay, $400,000 and we close in three weeks."

Now that is motivation! However, I still did not buy the home, because it did not fit my investment strategy. This house is still for sale. Now it's listed with a real estate company. The price is $449,000. The builder will be stuck with real estate fees. Would he have been better off making a deal with me for $375,000? What would you do?

Current Landlords

Sometimes you can find landlords who are looking to leave the rental business. They know the importance of cash flow and may be interested in helping you with financing. Also, since they are landlords, they're not as emotionally attached to a property as a homeowner.

Mobile Homes

New mobile homes bear little resemblance to the trailers of yesteryear. I know many investors who work this market very successfully.

Quick Tips

Manufactured home dealers can be very flexible with financing. If you live in the right area of the country, this may be a great way to start your investment career.

Get Started

Realtors

A crackerjack agent can be your most valuable resource in the hunt for good properties. Here are some tips for finding and developing a good working relationship with a realtor:

- Ask around in the professional community for recommendations, but also be willing to work with ambitious rookies.

- Ask someone who has taken a property off the market which agents call to inquire whether they would consider relisting with them.

- Negotiate a discounted commission schedule with an agent in exchange for listing other properties with him or her, and for referring other buyers and sellers.

- Sign a short-term listing agreement to motivate the agent to sell your property right away, that is, in not more than 90 days.

- Besides helping you find a suitable property, flexible realtors may be willing to help buyers finance part of the deal by lending them their commission fee, typically 5 to 7 percent of the purchase price. This amount could be your down payment.

- Find an agent who will not be embarrassed if you put in a low-ball offer. The seller may in fact be interested in ANY offer. Also avoid talkative brokers. Often they can talk themselves right out of a deal.

- The agent must be comfortable with allowing you to make your offer to the seller and their agent directly. If the agent wants to always present your offer for you, look elsewhere.

Working with Realtors

Many investors like to work with realtors. It saves them research time and foot-work. However, commissions are involved, and if you don't pick the right agent, you may lose out on deals. Most realtors do not understand the mind-set of investors. They sometimes won't allow you to do things, like make your own pre-sentations, and they act shocked when you come up with an offer that to them seems way out of line. Let me give you an example.

A Rookie Realtor

A very aggressive young realtor, better known as a "rookie," approached us about an investment property that had not yet been listed. The seller didn't want to move for at least nine months. The property was located in one of my "farming" areas, so I went to look. The real estate agent had no idea how much the seller wanted for the home—just that the seller wanted to sell privately without open houses and wanted to lease back until the seller was ready to move.

We asked for more information. I had already run comps on the neighborhood, so I knew what had sold recently and for how much. The real estate agent brought back this information:

- The sellers would not disclose a loan balance.

- They would not offer any owner financing.

- They were not interested in lease-optioning the property.

- They wanted $50,000 more than the most expensive property sold in that community.

So, what do you think of their motivation? There is none. I told the agent to call me in six months when they still haven't sold.

Quick Tips

Working with realtors takes time. You are trying to build a relationship and educate them about what you're looking for: price range, neighborhood, floor plan, etc. You also want them to understand that you must know everything about the property and the loan before you make any offers. If they are not willing to be that flexible, find another one.

One final note: In some areas of the country, where the economy has gotten a bit cooler, real estate companies are putting on seminars to try to teach people (of course, what they're really trying to do is sell) about real estate investing. Look at hungry companies like these when you are out and about.

Distressed Properties

These properties are often in the FSBO listings, but realtors also list them. In the listings, look for the phrases "handyman's special," "as is," or "needs work."

Private Auctions

Many sellers turn to private auction companies to liquidate their property. In the weeks before the auction, the auction company will schedule open houses. Look for ads in the local papers or ask a local realtor to find out about upcoming auctions. Most companies cooperate with realtors. Make sure you do your homework before you bid on auction properties. Call local auction companies (check the yellow pages and the Internet) and ask to be put on their mailing list for real estate auctions. Be well prepared before you attend one of these. Know the property, set your top price, and stick to it no matter what!

Partnership Disputes

Some great deals can arise when parties in partnerships disagree strongly enough to want out of the agreement. Most partnerships ultimately don't work out, so this can be a real opportunity to find bargains.

Property Financing Problems

An example of this is a borrower who is unable to make a balloon payment from a private lender, and the owner will not allow a modification to extend the contract. Your courthouse could be a good source of knowledge if it's computerized. If the borrower cannot sell the property in time to salvage the loan, the private lender has the right to foreclose.

Other Sources for Finding Property

- Homes for sale where sellers are moving up and need to sell their existing home first in order to qualify for a loan.
- Neighbors of your existing rental properties can often bring leads.

Partnership Opportunities

Having lived in the Rockies, I often get a chance to visit the mountains. Ski season in the winter is beautiful, but my favorite time of the year is summer. Hiking, horseback riding, walking quaint streets, and shopping are great pastimes.

When I visit mountain towns, I also visit the local real estate offices to get an idea of what mountain property is selling for. On one of my visits, I spoke with the owner of a local real estate company in Breckenridge. He asked if I would be interested in a partial ownership of a condo right off the best ski slope in town.

The condo was owned by a partnership. The person selling his interest had a falling out with two of the other partners and wanted out of the agreement. The condo was worth $600,000. He was willing to sell his quarter interest for $125,000, which was a $25,000 discount off his purchase price.

I looked at the condo and decided to pass. Yes, I could have owned a place in the mountains for only $125,000, but I didn't want the hassle of having to make scheduling arrangements with others. What if there were scheduling conflicts? Since I would have been the low man on the totem pole, I would probably have been given the worst weeks, like late fall when stores are closed and it's too cold to hike, or the spring "mud" season.

Don't Forget

Many investors buy into partnerships. If you're interested in investigating those opportunities, make sure a good real estate attorney reads over the partnership documentation as it relates to your investment. This is for your protection. Partnerships can be a good way to get a foothold in property that would otherwise be unaffordable.

Quick Tips

Pension plan tip: You can also have your self-directed IRA or self-directed 401(k) invest in these properties.

- Homeowner associations.
- Home builders in financial trouble.
- New custom homes under construction. Meet the prospective owners and ask what they are doing with their current house.
- Current landlords who are having a hard time renting out their properties. Check under "Houses for Rent" in the classifieds.
- Garage, moving, and estate sales.

Buying from Relocation Companies

Corporations that have to relocate their employees sometimes purchase the property the employees are living in if they've been unsuccessful in selling it themselves.

In one recent case, a couple had purchased a home in 1994 for $265,000. Their employer wanted to transfer them to the home office because one of them got a major promotion. They needed to sell their existing home to qualify for the new loan. The employer offered to buy the home if the property remained unsold, but also offered them a $15,000 bonus if they were able to sell it on their own.

The employee couldn't sell it. His original asking price was $434,000. The company received three independent appraisals, averaged them out, and offered the employee $407,000. This property is still sitting on the market at $397,000, with no offers. It is a lovely home, but it backs up to green storage units. Relocation companies need to get properties like these off of their books.

I have had three opportunities in the past five years to buy property through a relocation company. I took advantage of two. In both cases I bought them for more than $50,000 under the asking price.

Marketing

As an investor, you need several different ways of finding properties to buy. One way is direct marketing. Carefully thought-out marketing pieces can bring you leads that you might not otherwise get. I like to use simple brochures, flyers, door hangers, and various classified ads to bring my services to people's attention.

Also keep the following in mind: When someone reads your marketing material, the primary thought is, "What's in it for me?"

Get Started

How do you find these relocation companies?

Call the major corporations in your area and ask the employee benefits or human resources department which agent they use to help sell their employees' properties when the employees move. Call the real estate agent and ask them who the relocation company is for that particular corporation.

One property I purchased was listed through Coldwell Banker, but the relocation company was Cendant, which is the parent company of Coldwell Banker. The other property I purchased was through a company that has its own relocation department.

This is an excellent method for finding and negotiating properties well under fair market value. Who knows—you may be able to get financing thrown into the deal.

Get Started

Whether you're trying to find properties through a seller directly or go through a third party such as a real estate agent, your marketing piece must:

· Be directly targeted to the reader.

· Be easy for the reader to understand.

· Close with a next step or action follow-up.

Language is the decisive factor in advertising. Read the following two ads and see how one has more drawing power than the other. Which of these two ads would you be more likely to consider if you were a buyer?

FOR SALE BY OWNER

8 units—good area. Priced at $330,000.

Call Lisa @ 123–4567

OWNER MUST SELL

High income-producing 8-unit apartment building.

In prime rental area. Excellent condition.

Call Lisa @ 123–4567

Now consider these two additional ads:

I pay CASH

For your real estate equity if you are in foreclosure.

Call Lisa for a no-cost consultation. 123–4567

Sell me your home FAST . . . for CASH!

Any condition . . . as is.

Don't wait! Call Lisa while she's buying!

123–4567

You can do a direct mail campaign to probate, foreclosure, bankruptcy, and divorce attorneys. You need to let them know you're ready to make cash offers on any properties they need to divest.

Marketing Methods

Flyers

These can be distributed or posted anywhere and are a lot cheaper than direct marketing. Choose brightly colored paper and lively graphics. Here's something I have used:

WANTED

A House to Buy!

Are you planning to sell your home in the near future?

Do you want to save commission $$$ by selling it yourself?

I am not a real estate agent!

I am looking for a nice home in Southeast Fort Collins.

$165,000 – $200,000

Call Lisa, weekdays @ 123–4567

Door Hangers

These are inexpensive and have the additional advantage of getting you out into the neighborhoods where you want to buy to keep tabs on new developments there. You can also meet potential clients directly while making the rounds! Your door hanger message should read something like this:

CAN YOU HELP A FUTURE NEIGHBOR?

I am trying to find a 3 or 4 bedroom home

in your neighborhood.

I am not a real estate agent.

I help people live in good communities like yours.

If you know of anyone who is thinking of selling

CALL 123–4567

WE BUY REAL ESTATE AND PAY FINDER'S FEE FOR PROPERTIES!*

*Note: In some states, you cannot pay finder's fees. Check the state law before using this phrase.

Postcards

Postcards can be effective marketing and are also cheaper to mail than brochures or letters. But unless you are mailing them out in volume, and at least six times to the same address, I would recommend a brochure that answers the seller's immediate questions.

Letters or Brochures

Property owners usually have a lot of questions about selling their property to investors. You can answer most of these questions up front in a well-worded brochure or letter mailed directly to them. Be sure to include your business card.

The example is taken from a brochure that I have used successfully. It is in a simple Q/A format directed to an individual and, in closing, calls for action: "Pick up the phone and call us."

Dear Property Owner:

Are you currently facing any of these problems?

1. Your property has been on the market longer than a month with no interest.

2. You signed a 3-month listing agreement with a local real estate agent who has not seen your property since the night you signed the contract.

3. You are trying to sell your property on your own with no success.

4. A contract fell through due to the borrower being unable to qualify for a new loan.

If these or any other obstacles are barring sale of your property, we are your solution.

ABC Investments, Inc., a company that buys mortgages nationwide, has branched out into the local real estate market. What does this mean for you? We may be able to convert that FOR SALE property into a SOLD property FAST! We have cash to buy your home NOW! We have a variety of programs to offer that can sell your home quickly. Avoid real estate commissions, lenders' requirements, and other administrative hassles.

Here are some answers to commonly asked questions:

What type of real estate do you buy?

We look at any type of real estate from residential to soft commercial, apartments, student housing, even mobile homes on land.

What is your fast-track program?

If a property meets all of our evaluation criteria upon our inspection, and we put it under contract, the closing could occur when we get a title commitment. That is usually within seven business days.

How flexible are you?

We are very flexible. Say you are building a new home and need to stay in your existing home until completion. We can purchase your existing property and allow you to either rent back the home from us or we can negotiate the sale, allowing you to live there free until completion. We realize every person has needs, and we will work with you to do whatever it takes to help you solve your problem.

Who would do the closing?

We will be happy to work with your legal advisor or title company, or you can work with our professionals, as you desire.

What about closing costs?

Discussed on a case-by-case basis and are negotiable.

What if I am working with a real estate agent? How will that affect his listing?

We will look at the real estate, whether it is listed or not. If you do have a property listed with an agent, the agent is still entitled to his or her commission. You would have to speak with your real estate professional about their fees.

Is there real estate that you DON'T buy?

We don't buy gas stations, churches, taverns, hotels, or properties that are out of our level of expertise. We buy 99 percent of the types of real estate that are in the marketplace today.

I am behind in my payments. Can you help?

Yes, we buy properties of people who are delinquent or in foreclosure.

What is your next step?

Pick up the phone and call us today for a free evaluation of your property.

It's a Wrap

✔ Due diligence is a must before you buy any property.

✔ Mold must be disclosed.

✔ Properties can be found through many different means— find the ones that work for you.

✔ Marketing will help you find properties to purchase.

CHAPTER 6

How to Negotiate the Best Deals

Do I Need to Read This Chapter?

➡ Do you know the questions you need answered before you negotiate?

➡ Do you know the best way to ask those questions?

➡ You've never heard of rent-back opportunities.

➡ You've never heard of seller financing.

Negotiating the Deal

Not long ago I had an opportunity to tie up a property at 25 percent below market. I went through the property several times, trying to decide how much I would have to spend to make the floor plan more livable. The comps supported a much higher resale. But by the time I got around to presenting my offer, the house was under contract. The lesson here of course is, "He who hesitates, loses." I should have tied up the property immediately with a written contract. The fine points could have been worked out later, but some sort of written contract was necessary to keep it within my negotiation range.

Quick Tips

The key to negotiating a great deal is to get the seller's story. The more you know about the seller's motivation, the better you will be able to tailor your offer for acceptance. Know what the seller paid for the property so you have an idea of how much equity there is to play with. The courthouse can help you if you can't get the answer from the seller.

Get Started

Know Your Seller's Motivation

It is so important to determine the motivation of the seller before you make your offer. I feel that investors who don't understand the seller's motivation from the start do themselves an injustice. Let me illustrate the importance of discovering the seller's motivation by sharing a recent experience.

I recently moved to California. I had leased a property long enough to determine whether I would be happy there. Once I established that California was just fine with me, I needed to buy a house instead of rent. Taxes alone would make this a no-brainer. The prices of single family homes are almost double what they are in Colorado, where I had moved from. As you can imagine, this took a little getting used to.

I started looking at properties in the communities I was interested in. The next day I went back to look at two of them again. I had comps of the area and a good idea about what the properties were worth. As I was leaving property number one, the seller drove up. Without asking my realtor, I waited until the seller parked his car and went over to have a chat.

Here was how I discovered his motivation firsthand:

"I just toured your home for the second time," I said. "It's lovely. I especially enjoy the view and the quiet. Why are you moving?"

He said, "I recently got divorced and need to move to a smaller home in a less expensive area."

"When do you need to move?" I asked.

"I need to be out of here within the next 30 days."

I asked him where he was moving to. He had no idea. He hadn't begun his search for property. By now my realtor was getting anxious. I thanked the seller, told him I would like to think about the property some more and get back to him.

When I got in the car, I said to my realtor, "The seller is divorced, has no money, and has nowhere to live. He needs the equity in his home so he can move and get on with his life. I would be willing to make an offer that allows him to stay free in the property for an additional month after closing. This would give him time to find another place to live."

His property was a little under market to begin with. I felt confident I probably could have gotten an additional 5 percent discount. It would have been a win-win. If you don't know much about investing in California, know this: Properties often sell for much more than their asking price. Especially in desirable areas.

The second property I revisited was a beauty. Only on the market for 18 days, the seller had dropped her price. She left the home while my realtor and I toured the property. As we were getting ready to leave, she returned. Again, I wanted to find out why she was selling.

I started out talking about her furnishings, which were Japanese. I had recently been to Japan, so I was able to comment about some of the objects she had in her home. I discovered that she grew up in Japan and, even though she wasn't Japanese, considered Japan her home. We had quite the conversation. She and her husband were retiring to another area. He was already there remodeling their 100-year-old Victorian. She hated being in this home alone.

She had a ton of equity in the property. Her motivation was not to get top dollar, but to move as soon as possible. I ended up making an offer on this property that included a quick closing. Had I not spent the time getting to know her, I would never have learned her true motivation.

To get answers to the following questions, approach the topics in a nonintimidating manner:

- Why is the seller selling the property?
- What does the seller plan to do with the money?

- What is the real reason the owner is getting rid of the house?
- How long has the seller owned the property?
- Who actually owns the property?
- Is there a time frame in which the owner must sell?
- How long has it been on the market?
- How has the owner tried to sell it?
- What will happen to the property if the owner is unable to sell it?
- How did the seller settle on the asking price?
- Is there a mortgage, and if so, is it assumable?
- What is the balance on the loan?
- Will the owner consider financing the purchase?
- What will happen with the cash received from the sale?

The Negotiating Process

Never offer the asking price. The asking price is only the seller's first offer. In a slow market, you can always reduce the price, because the asking price is always inflated. You also want to get concessions from the seller, such as assistance with financing. Do your homework in advance; know what comparable properties have sold for.

Understand why the owner wants to sell. Divorce, relocation, or loss of a job can precipitate the sale of the home. So can retirement or a death in the family, but these factors affect the seller's emotional motivation differently. Perhaps the seller has bought another home and must sell his existing home as a contingency for qualifying for financing on the new home. If the seller is a landlord, he may just be burned out from property maintenance, tenant problems, and so on. Or he may be overextended financially and need to unload the property to remain solvent. The more you know about why the owner wants to sell, the better you can target your offer.

There are times when bargains are available in both price and terms. The best bargains come when the seller needs to sell quickly in a buyer's market. In those circumstances, a below-market offer will either be accepted or countered. Never be afraid to walk away from a deal. Your offer may in fact be the only one on the table, despite what the seller would have you believe. If you start to walk, a motivated seller will panic and reopen negotiations. That opens the door for you to gain more concessions. No two deals are exactly alike.

Get Started

Negotiate to Win

The following account illustrates how important it is to get the seller's story in the early stages of negotiating:

One day while walking my dog, I noticed a gentleman putting up a "For Sale by Owner" sign in his yard, so I walked over to talk with him. He and his wife were building an expensive new home, and the bank had granted them a loan contingent upon his selling this property. He had an 8 percent nonqualifying assumable loan on the property.

I offered to assume his loan and give him $10,000 over his loan balance. We wrote up a contract, but the bank turned it down. They said that since I was assuming the loan, he was still liable if I defaulted. The bank did not think he could afford the payments if this happened.

He thought our deal was over, but I went back and offered him a five-year lease on his property. The balance of his original loan would be paid down to the point where he could afford the payments if the property became vacant after five years. I then had a separate option agreement to buy the property from him after he closed on his new home, and let him rent back as my contribution to the option consideration. In other words, I put no option money down, and I let him live in his existing property rent free until he could move into the new one.

The bank was happy with the five-year lease and granted him the loan on his new property. As soon as they closed, I exercised my option and assumed his nonqualifying loan.

I rented the property only twice in the eight years I owned it. It was a great deal for me. I put $10,000 down and assumed the loan at $73,000. I sold it for $155,000. Ironically, one of the tenants had enough money set aside to buy the property instead of me, but opted to take the family on a cruise instead.

Rent-backs can make the deal for the seller. In the above case, the sellers didn't have to move twice. They knew the house was sold, so they could relax even if there were delays in moving to the new property. When you offer this kind of flexibility and willingness to work with sellers, they will be more receptive to price and other terms you may need. It's a win-win. Had the sellers sold the property for cash but had to move twice, they would have gotten more money but had a lot more aggravation.

Don't Forget

You never know what might be an acceptable offer until you actually make an offer. When people are motivated, amazing things can happen.

Seller Financing

This is a win-win deal if the presentation is right. In a seller-financed or purchase-money loan, the seller finances the buyer and, in effect, becomes the lender. Sellers will frequently carry the loan at a lower interest rate than hard moneylenders. If a seller is getting 3 percent in a savings account, he or she may be willing to carry a loan at 6 percent, even though the going mortgage rate is 7 percent. This is great for investors with a low down payment, since sellers will take back a first or second offer if they're motivated to get the property sold. Here's how to proceed:

- If the owner is willing to finance the sale, ask for no payment for at least six months. This gives you a cushion to either resell the property or fix it up for rental. Hopefully, the rental income will cover the owner-financed loan. What's the worst that could happen?

- Ask to put as little down as possible, again giving you the cash you need for repairs. This works well in negotiating rehab property. Some investors ask to put nothing down, but I think putting a little money on the table is a good faith gesture.

- Ask for a below-market interest rate and as long a term as possible (30 years or more).

- If this is a rental property, ask that the rent be included in your purchase price so you get credit for the next two or three months before closing. That means you get three months rent while it is the seller's responsibility to collect the payments.

  1. Require that everything stay with the property—carpet, windows treatments, appliances, air conditioners, etc.

  2. Tell the seller you would like to close as late as possible. If you're going to flip the property, a late closing gives you time to find another buyer.

  3. Ask the seller to pay all closing costs and the cost of title insurance.

  4. Ask the seller to pay for obvious repairs or give you a credit off the purchase price, so you can have these items repaired.

5. Always offer the lowest price possible, because every dollar off the purchase price is a dollar you save. But be fair; don't offer a price that insults the seller.

6. Every contract should contain a weasel or contingency clause that lets you legally back out of the contract should you decide not to go through with the purchase of the property. Here are the most common contingency clauses:

- Closing contingent on buyer's inspection and approval of condition of the property.
- Closing contingent on buyer obtaining financing at (whatever percent is desired) for 30 (or however many desired) years.
- Closing contingent on buyer's partner, spouse, or whoever's approval.
- Closing contingent on buyer's contractor inspection and approval.
- Closing contingent on buyer obtaining a home inspection report agreeable to buyer.
- Closing contingent on buyer's inspection and approval of all paperwork, leases, tenant histories, title work, and bids for repairs.

- Every written contract should have an expiration period that states that the contract will be voided in 24 or 48 hours, giving enough time for the seller to counter your offer but not enough time for your contract to be shopped by other realtors having their friends bid up the price.

Quick Tips

For holding property on a short-term basis, the seller may be willing to finance a short-term note so the investor has time to resell the property. Generally this would be offered as an interest-only loan at a higher rate of interest, with the balloon due at closing.

It's a Wrap

✓ Learn as much as you can about the seller.

✓ Never offer the asking price—you can probably reduce the price.

✓ Rent-backs can make the deal.

✓ Seller financing is great if it's handled correctly.

CHAPTER 7

Finding Money for Your Deals

Do I Need to Read This Chapter?

→ You don't know all of the financing options available to you.

→ You don't know how many different mortgage options exist.

→ You've never heard of portfolio lenders.

→ Unconventional financing options never occurred to you.

→ You're interested in using IRAs and other retirement funds to finance your purchase.

Financing

To be a successful real estate investor, you need to know how to find good deals and how to find money for these good deals.

The sources for funds are almost limitless. You can borrow from banks, mortgage companies, or portfolio lenders. You may need to explore alternatives, like borrowing from family members, friends, or other investors who are interested in a healthy return on an investment. You can refinance other property, pulling equity out for investing. You can take out a home equity loan on your primary residence, get a line of credit from the bank, and so on. You can even buy property with credit cards, although that's very risky!

Borrowing money can be risky for the fledgling real estate investor. Every loan must be paid back—even loans to friends and family. Late payments can affect your credit. Further, if you can't pay them back at all, you may be forced into bankruptcy. Missing payments to a private investor can also be as damaging, especially if you're trying to build a long-term relationship.

Minimize your risk by having a cushion of savings to fall back on if something goes wrong. Obviously, make sure that your investment will bring you positive cash flow.

Mortgages

To get a mortgage, you have to go through a credit check with one of the three national credit reporting agencies: Equifax, TransUnion, or Experion. The credit report produces a rating called a FICO score. Anything over 700 is considered a good credit risk.

The lender wants verification of income, employment, and any other passive income to prove you can make the payments and support the investment property. Even though they know you will be renting the property out, the bank only gives you 75 percent credit for each payment. This allows 25 percent toward vacancies, upkeep, taxes, and insurance.

You could also buy a property to live in, getting an owner-occupied loan. You must live on the property for a least one year before converting it to a rental. This reduces your interest rate on the loan.

Now let's look at the wide array of mortgages that are available. Some will suit your purposes and some won't.

Blanket Mortgage

A blanket mortgage gives you coverage of all or more than one of your properties, and allows you to use equity on all of your financing. If you have trouble qualifying for a new loan and have other assets, a blanket mortgage allows you to tap into those other assets for a new loan. The downside is that you tie up your assets and put your other properties at risk.

Get Started

Lenders Make the Rules, Investors Follow Them

- Lenders require independent property appraisals—estimates of worth from someone other than self-interested owners or perspective owners. Lenders select appraisers, and investors (typically) pay for the reports.

- Lenders want credit checks from credit-reporting agencies. Generally, investors pay for these reports.

- Loans are not issued unless the debt is secured with property and recorded at the courthouse.

- Lenders generally do not make a 100 percent loan-to-value loan unless a third party is involved, like the VA, or a private mortgage insurer guarantees or insures a portion of the loan.

- Lenders do not make loans unless the debt is secured by both the value of the property and your willingness to be personally liable for the debt.

- Investors don't get financing unless they are willing to maintain fire, theft, and liability insurance throughout the mortgage term.

- Lenders do not make a loan without clear and marketable title, unless the state prohibits the sale of title insurance. In its place, owners can buy state-sponsored protection.

- Your FICO (credit) score is everything!

Don't Forget

Many successful real estate gurus say, "I'll pay your price if you let me set the terms." Though private financing is an excellent way to buy property, let me caution you. Never pay more than what the property is worth, even if the owner is willing to finance you. If the property drops in value, or you end up in a negative cash-flow situation because you can't rent the property for the payment you owe, you could be in big trouble.

Blend Mortgage

This allows you to merge a new loan with an existing one. Normally, the interest rate from both loans is blended to arrive at the interest rate for the new loan. The merging of the two loans often produces an overall lower rate. Blended mortgages offer the option of creative financing. The buyer may be able to assume the seller's existing low-interest loan.

Graduated Mortgage Payment

A GMP has reduced payments initially, with increases over a predetermined schedule. Then payments level off for the rest of the load period. This is a good way to go if you think your income will increase over time. Another benefit is that it is easier to qualify for a larger loan, since the payments start out smaller. The downside is negative amortization. Because the interest you are saving is added to the mortgage, you could end up owing more than what a simple loan would have cost.

Graduated Payment Adjustable Mortgage

This is similar to a GMP, except that the initial low payments are graduated in years two, three, and four, and in year five the loan is accelerated (balloon payment).

Pledged Account Mortgage

The buyer puts a down payment of 10 percent or more into a pledged savings account.

Adjusted or Variable Rate Mortgage

Payments are indexed to the current interest rate, and the loan interest rate is adjusted yearly. This is great if interest rates are low, but could get you into trouble if interest rates go up. However, I recently learned that when lenders do the adjustments, they change more than the interest rates. They also check that the monthly payments will pay off the loan at the end of the original 30-year period, neither sooner nor later. If you can prepay a little principal each month, the lender must reduce the required mortgage payments to make the loan last the full 30 years of its original term.

Rollover Mortgage

The borrower and lender agree to a 15- or 30-year repayment schedule, during which time the mortgage is renegotiated or "rolled over" at regular intervals. This is great for the lender if interest rates increase. The buyer can always refinance.

FHA and VA Mortgages

Check with your institution on whether you qualify for these low-down- or no-down-payment loans. They are government secured.

Assumable Mortgages

Back in the old days, finding nonqualifying assumable loans was easy. You still can find loans that are assumable, if you can qualify for them from the bank that has the original loan. Lenders do have the right to increase your interest rate on assumption. When you assume a loan, you are taking over the seller's payments from what he owes the bank. If you have available cash and want to obtain a lower interest rate, this option may work for you. You do have to pay off the equity difference to the seller unless he is willing to seller-finance that difference.

Wraparound Mortgages

A wraparound is seller-financing, where a new loan is written to cover the existing loans plus the seller's equity. It allows the borrower to take title to the property by combining a first and a second and "wrap" them together. The seller makes payment on the first and pockets any spread difference between the first and your payment. A wrap can get you into a property with the potential for a lower interest rate. It is also a safeguard for the seller, since he knows when you have not paid the mortgage. He still pays on his first and can institute foreclosure if you become in serious default.

Quick Tips

A Graduated Payment Plan

One of my tenants wanted to buy my rental. The amount he wanted to pay for the property was agreeable. He only had a small down payment, but was willing to make graduated monthly payments so the loan would pay off in seven years.

Eventually, we converted the house to a lease-option plan. When he had raised the down payment that was sufficient for the loan (this took a year), he exercised the option and started making payments. With each year, he made an additional principal payment, and his monthly payment went up. This is the last year of his loan payment, and he has paid like clockwork.

Graduated payments can work in a variety of ways. This is just one way in structuring a deal with increases each year.

Get Started

Choosing a Financing Plan

Here are some points to consider when choosing a financing plan:

Put as little down as possible—5 percent down is good. If the property goes up 5 percent in value in the first year, you've make 100 percent on your investment.

Always have cash reserves. This can be anything from a mutual fund to a CD, as long as it's something that's easy to convert to cash should you need it.

Consider having a line of credit. This is credit provided through a bank that you can draw on as needed. Drawing a line from a home you occupy is called a home equity loan. There are also other types of lines of credit where investment property and other collateral can be hedged.

Mortgage Hypothecation

If you own a home or other real estate that has substantial equity, it is possible to offer the seller of an investment property a second mortgage on your other real estate.

A great source for a loan is an institution that is a portfolio lender. These are banks that keep their own loans, that is, they don't sell on the secondary market. If you can demonstrate you're a worthy borrower, they may make a loan for you. World Savings and Washington Mutual are examples of such institutions. Washington Mutual, now the largest lender in the country, recently offered a 1 percent-down mortgage loan program for owner occupants. Most portfolio lenders are very picky about giving loans on mixed-use properties (such as condos upstairs with retail stores below). To find out who is a portfolio lender in your area, ask a good local mortgage broker who represents many companies. They will know who does well with investor loans.

I have also found that Wells Fargo (which, to my knowledge, is not a portfolio lender) has always tried to go the extra mile for some of my loan applications.

Owner-financing is an ideal way to get into the real estate without points, fees, and other expenses, as well as offering a favorable interest rate.

Credit cards: It can be done, but understand that this is a very expensive and risky way to go. Exhaust other possibilities first.

Finance companies, along with credit cards, are the choice of last resort. Finance companies charge very high rates of interest, making it hard to be profitable over the long term.

FHA 303(k) loans are a good product for rehabbers. The loans are given in two parts. One part pays the seller, the other is held in escrow until the property is fixed up. Look into this program if you are a rehabber.

Cash value in your life insurance policy. If your whole life policy is more than six years old, you may be able to borrow against it to buy real estate. Check with your insurance agent to see if you would qualify and what the rules and payback periods are.

If you have substantial assets tied up in stocks, bonds, and mutual funds, you may be able to borrow against this collateral. If you don't pay, the investor has the right to take the stock.

You can take out a second mortgage on your primary residence, also known as a home equity loan, to help you raise cash reserves.

You can use private mortgages that you own as down payment money for another property.

Your retirement plan can buy real estate if it is a self-directed IRA or qualified plan.

Charge It!

I have a friend in New Mexico who bought a foreclosure by maxing out all of her and her husband's credit cards. She felt the property was a bargain in a beautiful setting, and that after she fixed it up a bit, she would make a fortune.

She began rehabbing the property and soon discovered she would have to spend more money then she had planned. At 21 percent interest, she was close to filing bankruptcy. To avoid this, she and her husband decided to sell their existing house and live in the rehab. The cash from the sale of their old home paid off the credit cards.

She still lives in the rehab six years later! So much for her single-family investing career. She now only does mobile homes. She says it's a lot easier to charge a mobile home than a single family home.

Loans

The following types of loans are available if you require some flexibility: Condo and townhouse loans, kiddie condo loans, fixer-upper loans, convertible loans (going from an adjustable to fixed-rate loan, loans where the borrower has filed bankruptcy, and so on) are all considerations for flexible lenders.

100 Percent Loan

Another party provides the down payment in a CD that the bank holds as collateral. The bank receives the interest. If the parties involved default, the bank has the right to dip into the CD.

Low Documentation Loans

A lot of self-employed people need low documentation loans to get into a property. Assets and employment are minimally documented, provided the borrower puts up a larger down payment—anywhere from 25 to 30 percent down.

Smaller Down Payment Investor Loans

You can get investor loans out in the marketplace with as little as 10 percent down. Institutions usually require more down, since the property is non-owner-occupied. A flexible lender has the ability to make exceptions. You would probably have to pay a premium to get this kind of loan.

Foreign Nationals

Portfolio lenders offer adjustable rate loans to foreign nationals, provided they have a green card and a significant down payment.

Helping Out the Folks

Professional friends of mine have parents who are trying to buy a property. They don't have the down payment money, but their income can qualify them for a loan. So the parents asked the children for help.

The institution the parents were going through did not want the down payment gifted to the parents. So what my friends did was put the down payment in a CD that the bank holds as collateral. My friends receive the interest on the CD. If the parents default on the loan, the bank has the right to dip into the CD for the amount in default.

The parents got their home, my friends were able to help their parents, they receive interest on this CD until the parents pay down that portion of the loan, and the bank felt adequately collateralized. Another win-win financing deal!

Dealing Successfully with Institutional Lenders

- Try to develop a long-term relationship with at least two bankers locally who handle real estate loans. Take them to lunch. Show them your business plan. Let them know what you are trying to accomplish. Let them get to know you.

- Remember that banks, credit unions, and savings and loans companies all have the same objective—to make safe, secure loans. The more supporting documents you can provide, the more likely you are to convince them that making a loan to you is a safe proposition.

- Don't lie to the lender. If you are buying an investment property, tell them up front. (You will be surprised about how little the percentage point difference is between an investor loan and an owner-occupied property loan.) All institutional lenders are government insured. If you have an owner-occupied loan on a rental property and you are discovered, you may have to answer not just to the lender but also to the Treasury Department.

- Watch out for points and fees. Lenders easily increase their profit this way.

- If you are buying a property to flip, consider a bridge loan or short term (under six months) of private financing, allowing you enough time to flip out the property. Be aware that if you don't sell the property within the six months, the bank will convert this to a fixed loan, which probably will have a higher rate attached to it. This type of loan is available from commercial lenders.

- Having another source of income like a steady job makes it easier for you to get a loan. Lenders like having more than one source of income from which the loan will be repaid, and being employed gives you more credibility.

- Having two phone numbers (your job and your home) and two addresses makes your loan application look more professional to the underwriters, even if you are self-employed.

- Make sure there is no prepayment penalty in the loan. If you have the money to pay off the loan, you should be able to do so without a penalty.

Unconventional Financing

Contract for Deed, Agreement for Deed, Land Contract

This is essentially a private installment purchase plan between two individuals. It protects the seller, since the deed is not given over until all payments are made. It has been used as a vehicle around the due-on-sale clause. Of course, if the seller is a scam artist, he could turn around and resell the property. Since the note is not recorded, the buyer would have no recourse. Due on sale can still be exercised if the lender finds out there was a sale. Only a title opinion can be given; no title insurance is possible, since the seller does not want the sale recorded.

Private Pension Funds and Foundations

Each plan typically has a trustee who runs it, usually an officer of the company or someone sitting on the board of directors of the foundation. Many people use other people's pension plans and charitable foundations to borrow money.

Moving a Mortgage

Many people, especially retirees, like mortgages. They like the steady payments to supplement their income. If, because of a sale or a refinance, you will be paying off a loan on which you have faithfully made payments to the seller, consider asking them if they would like to transfer the mortgage to another property you own or are buying. Do not offer to increase the interest rate to do this. If you have made payments in a timely manner and the sellers have enjoyed the monthly income, they might be receptive to the idea of continuing this arrangement.

Buying Property with a Private Mortgage Note

I found a property for sale that was free and clear. When I sat down with the seller, she was agreeable to owner-financing but wanted some cash as a reserve.

I had a note on a property in Boulder, Colorado, at the time the number one area of real estate appreciation in the United States. The face of the note was $100,000. The property I wanted to buy from the seller cost $122,000. I offered her the $22,000 down in cash, and she agreed to take the note for payments on the Boulder property.

I paid $78,000 for this note. I was able to get full face value at $100,000. In effect, I was into the property at $100,000 total for a $122,000 property, a discount of $22,000 to me because I used a note instead of cash.

This was a great deal for her, since she was getting income at 10 percent interest off the note that she could not get elsewhere.

Quick Tips

Buying properties with private mortgage notes you purchased at a discount is a great way to get financed and take advantage of getting 100 cents on the dollar for something you paid less for.

Long-Term Seller Financing

Many owners will finance the sale of a property to you if you can prove that you are a good credit risk. When you think about it, what is the worst that could happen if a buyer simply stops making payments on a property?

That worst case is that the seller has to foreclose, take the property back, and resell it. Remember, they got a down payment, a series of monthly payments (assuming that is how you structured the loan), and the property has probably either remained the same or gone up in value.

Once this system is explained to owners—especially those with a lot of equity or a free and clear property—they realize that unless they need the immediate cash, this is not a bad deal. In most cases, sellers want a decent interest rate so they're making money on these payments. Interest rates are negotiable. It depends on the deal. If you were to be financed on a property for 30 years at 1 point over the current interest rates, would this be worth it to you?

Anytime I have ever been involved in an owner-financed transaction, we were able to work out a fair and reasonable financing structure for both parties. Seller financing works, no matter what the economy. As a matter of fact, if the economy is in a downturn or interest rates go up, seller financing can become more commonplace. So when you make offers, always ask if the seller is willing to finance the sale and what terms would be necessary for them to do so.

Subordination

The seller not only finances the buyer, but agrees that his or her lien is secondary or subordinate to another loan.

For example, assume that an owner agrees to sell you a lot for $100,000 with $10,000 down and to subordinate the mortgage for $90,000. You could not go to a conventional lender and ask to borrow $200,000 for a building loan. As far as the lender is concerned, you would be asking for two-thirds of the loan because the lot, in the lender's thinking, is free and clear. The lender, by giving you a $200,000 loan, would have both the land and building as collateral under the first mortgage. You have used the lot seller's equity to finance your loan, even though you have not paid for the lot.

No Money Down

No money down deals work under the right set of circumstances, but it's not easy to negotiate with the seller to sell you the property with no money down and payback in monthly installments. The seller needs to be pretty motivated to do this.

Ruth Mary

Several years ago I came across a property for sale. The seller was recently widowed. She had lived in the house for 40 years and was moving into an assisted living facility. She owned the property free and clear and was willing to finance the sale and receive monthly income. I went to her realtor's office to make my presentation with my realtor in tow. This was my original offer:

Sales Price: $118,000 (full price offer)

Down Payment: $18,000

$1,000 per month for 100 months

Immediately, her real estate agent starts punching the numbers into his HP12C. "That's only $92,367 for the property," he said. "You're not even paying her interest"

I spoke to the widow directly. I asked her if she wanted interest on her money, and if so, what would be fair. She said 5 percent would be fair. I thought her realtor was going to have a heart attack right in his own office. Here was the deal that closed:

Sales Price: $118,000

Down Payment: $18,000

$100,000 @ 5% interest for 30 years

If you take out your HP12C and figure what my payment is, you'll see that I'm coming out way ahead. I didn't have to pay $1,000 per month. My payment is close to half that amount. I currently rent this property for $1,400. This will be the last loan I pay off, since it's at 5 percent.

Quick Tips

I paid full price, but I got my terms. Always try to give the seller what they want. If there are any concessions that need to be made, the seller should feel like you treated them fairly and with respect. I like buying property from retirees or people who have lived in the same property for a long time, because they tend to be more open to some form of owner-financing.

The Doctor

Jim, a bright young physician, and his bride were looking for property near the hospital where he worked. They had some savings, but weren't sure what they could afford.

They found a 100-year-old Victorian home within walking distance of the train station that would get Jim to work in 20 minutes. No stress, no tolls, no parking. They liked the home, but it needed work. Jim's credit union offered him an 80 percent loan on the property "as is." They planned to use their savings to get the property into move-in condition.

They asked the seller to carry a 20 percent second mortgage against the property. This loan would amortize over 30 years and balloon in five years with a 10 percent interest rate. The seller was thrilled with the full price offer and was happy to take a second for the new doctor.

Jim figures they will have rehabbed the property within three years and then can decide if they should stay or leave.

No money down deals work well when a property is in poor condition, since the seller can see that fix-up will be needed on the part of the buyer. The risk with no money down deals tends to be higher than it used to be. When real estate appreciates in leaps and bonds year after year, investors can enter into highly leveraged deals and come out okay. The same deal in a stable or sluggish economy rarely works. Based on recent activity and the economy, I would stay away from no money down deals. No equity makes you a poor risk to the seller.

Private Investors

Tap into your private sources. Relatives, friends, local stockbrokers, and other professionals may be interested to know that you are a real estate investor who is looking for a financial partner to buy and either resell or hold real estate. Real estate investor clubs are another good source of networking for money. (For a complete listing of clubs around the country, check out the National Real Estate Investors Association Web site. Contact persons and phone numbers are listed for every state.) If you already own some real estate that you used your own money on, private investors will be more interested in lending money to you with a decent return.

Investor relationship guidelines:

- Have a written agreement so you don't have to renegotiate your arrangement every time you seek capital from an investor.

- Be sure your relationship with your investor is nonexclusive so you aren't tied to a single investor.

- Have a clear understanding of how much money the investor has available for your venture. This way you can research properties that are within your reach and avoid wasting your efforts on ones that are not.

- Be sure you have quick, easy access to the cash so you can move fast on properties. Often, how quickly you can close the deal determines whether or not you get the property.

Granola Bob

I met Bob at a private mortgage seminar. He came to visit in 1992, six months after I had moved to Colorado. Bob is a sophisticated investor from California with 30-plus years of experience. He saw real potential in the tiny community of Fort Collins, Colorado, where the median priced home at the time was below the national average.

Bob wanted me to be his real estate agent and find properties for him to buy. He offered me a $750 finder's fee per deal. After negotiating for hours, we settled on being partners.

We agreed that I would find the property, negotiate with the seller, draw up a contract subject to Bob's approval, give him details on the property so we could make the right decisions and Bob could come up with the cash that was needed to close. Bob would provide the financing. Once the property closed, I'd put a tenant into the property and manage it. Anything over and above our debt and operating expenses, we would split 50–50. We would evaluate the situation after five years. If one of us wanted out, we would sell the property and split any profit 50–50.

What did Bob get? The opportunity to make money off his money, appreciation potential (which he got plenty of, since our partner properties doubled in value over the last 10 years), and monthly income over and above the debt on the property. I got the ability to get half ownership of these properties with no financial investment—only sweat equity. You decide: Was my return enough?

Private investors can be the key to your wealth accumulation. . . if you can work together compatibly.

P.S.: We call him Granola Bob because he was a strict vegetarian. On one of his visits he wanted to go hiking. When I dropped him off at the destination he requested, we saw a large herd of wild buffalo grazing nearby. This did not faze Bob. He thought he was safe because he was a vegetarian. A great mind for investing, but what a granola head!

- Your agreement should allow access to capital for repairs and renovations on homes you purchase.

- If you share each deal's profits with your investor, try to negotiate for no interest due on the money used for purchasing the property.

- An investor should let you do what you do without constantly interfering or requiring an unreasonable level of handholding.

- If you're not positive that the deal you are doing is a great deal, pass on using an investor. The worst thing that could happen is that you lose them money.

- Have an understanding with your investor that if he or she lacks capital or wants to pass on a deal, your investor will introduce you to others who are potential investors.

- Unless you have five people ready and able to fund your deals on a moment's notice, you should always be seeking out fresh investment capital and better terms for yourself.

- Keep your investors informed. Create a file that includes:

  - Photos of the property inside and out.

  - Expected purchase price.

  - Value of the property in terms of rental income or resale. Include a copy of the appraisal if you have one.

  - Required repairs and renovations, and your estimates of the amount of time and money needed to finish the job.

  - Capital required from the investor to put the deal together.

  - Expected return on the investment.

Don't Forget

The key to working with investors is to create win-win situations on each deal that you do together. You can do this by presenting a very professional and knowledgeable image and by keeping your investors informed of your real estate activities. Not every investor is an asset; know when and how to dissolve a relationship if it becomes burdensome.

It's important that your attorney draw up any documents pertaining to the private investor relationship so that all parties are comfortable. This would include partnership agreements and other entities. Make sure that there is a way for a partner to get out of a deal if he or she desires.

Hard Money Loans

There are lenders and private individuals that make short-term, high-interest rate loans to flippers, rehabbers, and real estate investors. You can find these private lenders in the classified ads under financing. Also, realtors, attorneys, title companies, and loan officers can direct you to them. Hard money is not cheap money. Interest rates of 15 percent or more are not uncommon. They also charge points and other fees. You are not likely to get a hard-money loan if you're looking to borrow more than 70 percent loan-to-value. Try to stay under 60 percent if you can.

Quick Tips

Hard money is short-term, high-interest financing used primarily for "find, fix, and flip" deals. It is often more flexible than standard banking institutions. Loans are made based on the future value of the property as estimated in a "subject to" appraisal and detailed rehab estimate.

Equity Sharing

A couple wanting to own a home has the income, but no down payment. Rather than waiting years to accumulate the down payment, an investor (in many cases a family member) puts up the down payment and closing costs. The couple pays the mortgage, taxes, and insurance, and pays back the investor over time. The equity share agreement has some expiration period attached to where the property is sold and the appreciation is split.

Roth IRA

A landlord named Maureen needed to raise $10,000 to pay off the IRS. Her tenant had just renewed his lease for $1,000 per month. The tenant had lived in that property for three years and had always paid rent promptly.

Maureen approached me asking where she could quickly raise the $10,000. I made the following deal with her: I opened the Lisa Moren IRA and wrote out a check to Maureen for $10,000. Thereafter, for 12 months, the $1,000 rent payment was made out to the Lisa Moren IRA. I received $1,000 per month for 12 months, tax-free. Not a bad return.

This type of agreement works well in markets where there is a lot of appreciation, such as California. The key to success in this arrangement is the coinvestors, the correct property, and a suitable agreement between the co-owners.

Retirement Funds

Are you aware that you can buy property with your IRA or 401(k)? You can also make loans, buy leases, and invest in other asset-based investments.

What you need is a custodian who allows you to self-direct your IRA or 401(k) to purchase these investments. The custodian keeps copies of all original documents in a fireproof vault. They prepare statements so you can see what assets are in your IRA, broken down by real estate as well as cash, stocks, and other securities. I am currently affiliated with the Entrust Group, which is the best custodian I can recommend. They sell no securities or investment products and have been in this business since 1981.

Quick Tips

If you want to learn more about doing deals with your IRAs or 401(k)s, log onto www.iraplus.com.

OPI: Other People's IRAs

I have a friend who uses the company Other People's IRAs to buy nice properties in nice neighborhoods, then turns around and puts the tenant on a five-year lease-option plan. He helps them improve their credit so they can afford to exercise the option and get a loan.

How does he do this?

He looks at their credit history and puts them on a budget.

If they pay timely, he gives them a bonus in the form of one month's rental payment per year toward the purchase price of the home.

At the end of year three, he pulls their credit to see if it has improved. If not, he warns them to "get it together" or forfeit their option consideration. He offers them an early out, keeping a small portion of the option consideration if he doesn't think they will be bankable within a year.

If they still elect to stay and are not bankable at the end, they forfeit the entire option, which goes to my friend.

What does he get?

- A significant option payment—a minimum of 10 percent or the agreed purchase price.
- The right to increase the rent every year.
- The right to boot out the tenant for nonperformance.
- He buys the properties with other people's IRAs, pays them interest, and produces cash flow every month without a dime of his own money from the tenant's lease payments.
- When the tenant does buy the property, it is at an agreed price from which my friend earns a nice profit.
- He gets to keep the option consideration as his fee. He receives a profit from some of the appreciation (he splits with the IRA holders).

What do the IRA holders get?

- Tax-deferred; tax-free income in the form of interest every month, secured by a note and deed of trust on the property.
- Diversification of their IRA portfolio.
- Appreciation potential, since my friend gives the IRA a piece of the appreciation as incentive to borrow the money.

Managing the Risks

You can manage the risks of high-leverage financing by following these five investment practices:

- Buy bargain-priced properties.
- Buy properties that you can profitably improve. Add sweat equity to update.
- Buy properties with low-interest financing, such as mortgage assumption, adjustable rate mortgages, buy-downs, or seller financing.
- Buy properties in up-and-coming neighborhoods that are soon to be revitalized.
- When all else fails to reduce the risk of high leverage to a comfortable level, increase your down payment to achieve a lower loan-to-value ratio and lower your monthly mortgage payments.

Simple ways to reduce your risk to leveraging exist. Start by maintaining an adequate amount of reserve capital for unexpected needs. Establish a line of credit so you're not scrambling for a loan when a heating system goes out. Consider establishing a corporate structure for your real estate holdings. Don't sign any documents until you understand them completely. Build a relationship with at least one good attorney and one tax expert.

Mortgage clauses can affect your investment decisions. Be sure you understand what you're getting into and how you'll pay for it before you make your final decision on how a property will be financed.

Get Started

 Guidelines for Obtaining a Real Estate Loan

· Prepare a good business plan for the property you want to buy. Submit this plan along with your loan application.

· Apply to a suitable real estate lender. Do your homework with the institution so that you know what they'll lend on before you submit your application.

· Be certain the amount of money you seek is acceptable to the lender. Know their guidelines.

· Never submit a handwritten loan application. Make sure it's typed.

· Don't bug your lender for a response. Give them time to study your application. This is especially important if you want to keep borrowing from the same lender.

· With income properties, be sure your debt cover ratio is 1.5 or higher. Lenders love higher ratios because it makes them feel safer. Every lender loves safety.

· Supply information about other income you have.

· Get the seller to take a second mortgage for your down payment, and you make monthly payments on the loan from the property income. This gives you 100 percent financing. Get your attorney to prepare a "reverse flip" agreement, where the seller receives credit for all payments you have made if you default on the loan. This offer makes a seller feel comfortable with taking out a second (or home equity loan) mortgage for your down payment.

· Have a cosigner ready if needed.

· Be ready to accept the lender's terms of the loan, interest rate, duration, and so on.

Develop Relationships with Bankers

To work with local banks, you must have a good business plan that bankers understand. They need to know what you're trying to accomplish, how much money you need, and how they'll be repaid. I have included a copy of both a business plan (Appendix A) and a marketing plan (Appendix B) for your reference.

Quick Tips

How do you develop a good relationship with lenders?

- Get to know the bank's lending procedures.

- Get involved in the community. A lot of lenders devote community time with the local Chamber of Commerce or Rotary Club. Get referrals from other professionals to a particular person at the local bank. An attorney or CPA can be a good source of recommendations.

- Make an appointment and present yourself to the banker. Bring pictures of properties you have already purchased. If you're just getting started, give them some background that will build your credibility.

- In most cases, institutional lenders limit the number of investment properties. Ask what the limit with that particular institution is, and if they make exceptions.

- As you get more involved in real estate investing and are making money, don't be surprised if one day a banker approaches you on his own for advice or looking to partner a deal with you. This happens.

- Always act professionally and be enthusiastic and willing to do what it takes to do the deal. A lender has to do his due diligence. That is required by regulators. In a borderline situation, where your ratios are close, ultimately your attitude can win the financing.

Preparations for Closing

Once negotiations have ended and a contract has been agreed upon, you need to prepare for the final closing. Always involve a title company or an attorney when closing. Make sure you have replacement value insurance on your property. If the property appreciates over time (and that, of course, is your aim), you need to be certain you are fully covered against disasters. Without replacement insurance, you could suffer substantial losses.

Don't Forget

What to do after the closing:

1. Put all utilities in your name until you have rented the property, provided it is a vacant property.

2. Make sure all utility and water companies have you listed on their records by property address. If a tenant does not pay, these companies will notify you. In some cases city governments have the right to put a lien on your property for nonpayment of bills. In a Colorado winter, no heat can be a disaster.

3. Obtain copies of any covenants or restrictions in the neighborhood for the property. Know what your tenants can and cannot do according to the neighborhood association rules. Make sure your tenants have a copy of these covenants.

4. Have adequate replacement value insurance on the property. Friends of mine in Texas had a rental that a careless tenant burned to the ground. To have another similar house built, it cost them $50,000 over what the insurance allowed.

It's a Wrap

✓ Minimize risk by having a cushion of savings to fall back on.
✓ There are many types of mortgages out there—choose the one that works for you.
✓ Put as little down as possible.
✓ Consider some unconventional financing options.
✓ Retirement funds can be used to finance real estate purchases.
✓ Develop good relationships with lenders.

CHAPTER 8

How to Manage Your Properties

Do I Need to Read This Chapter?

→ You need to know what your management responsibilities might entail.

→ You want to sustain a positive cash flow.

→ You think you might have to hire a property manager.

→ What's an appropriate rent?

→ You don't know how to screen potential tenants.

→ You have to prepare a lease agreement.

→ What resources are available to a landlord?

Property Management

Rental property can be financially rewarding in the following ways: It provides immediate cash flow, it provides a tax shelter that lowers your income, and it is an asset that appreciates in value over time.

Owning rental property, of course, also means that you must manage it, or pay someone else to do so. Many investors complain that being a landlord is a huge hassle. Here are the top five issues property owners most frequently face:

- Tenants who trash properties and still expect their security deposits to be returned to them.
- Vacancies, which create negative cash flow.
- Tenants who are late with their rental payment every month or who refuse to pay the rent, which necessitates eviction.
- Costly, unexpected major repairs that have to be done NOW.
- Complaints from the neighbors about tenant behavior.

Good property management solves most of these complaints. Successful "landlording" demands a willingness to handle problems immediately before they escalate into bigger problems. And the key to it all is attracting solid tenants who are responsible about caring for your property and paying their rent on time. If you are careful to explain exactly what is expected of your tenants before they move in, most problems will be eliminated. Of course, you also have to be willing to evict tenants when necessary.

Quick Tips

How do you know if your marketplace is a good area for rental property? Do a tenant analysis. First, check under "houses for rent" in the classified ads. Go back at least one month in your research to determine which areas of town seem to have frequent vacancies. Don't buy property in those areas. Call property managers to see what is available in your area and what they are asking in rent. Get a real estate agent to do a comparative market analysis. This will give you a good idea of what is active and sold in the neighborhoods you are farming.

To determine whether your investment will pay off in a positive cash flow, figure out your price-to-rent ratio. A good rule of thumb is the 1 percent rule. For example, a property should bring $2,000 on a $200,000 house. If interest rates are lower, you can adjust this to .75 percent. If rates are higher, adjust to 1.25 percent. If you can't cash-flow the home, you'd be better off passing on that property and finding one that is more financially promising.

Get Started

Sustaining Positive Cash Flow

- Insist on timely payment of rent and all other fees due to you.

- Impose fees on late payments.

- Raise rents every year to keep pace with inflation.

- Increase your cash flow with surcharges on pets, additional services, new appliances, etc.

- Borrow against your equity if you need cash, instead of taking it out of savings. Leverage.

- Watch your costs on property maintenance. Buy in bulk for multiple properties.

 - Keep an updated call list of prospective tenants.

- Refinance your mortgage if the savings on your monthly payments are enough to justify the points you pay.

- Take advantage of appealing property taxes on your rentals.

Don't Forget

Your basic rental expenses will comprise principle and interest on your loan, plus taxes and insurance. In addition, you need to factor in maintenance costs. Buying newer properties helps you avoid large costs in rehab and replacement. Vacancy represents negative cash flow. A good landlord does a great job of keeping prospective tenants in the pipeline. You should experience no more than a two- to four-week vacancy between tenants. Keep in mind that you're better off searching out the right person who will mean less headaches than snapping up the "bargain" that has the potential of becoming a "money pit."

Landlord vs. Property Manager

Once you own your property, you have a choice of being a landlord yourself or contracting with a property management company or an individual. There are pros and cons to going with a property manager. On the plus side, a property manager will:

- Find tenants, show your property, and negotiate leases
- Collect rents
- Pay bills and mortgage payments
- Keep bookkeeping records
- Send you a monthly accounting statement
- Make certain the building and grounds are properly maintained
- Contract for any major repairs or replacements that may be needed (with your authorization)
- Keep files on potential tenants

On the other hand, a property manager:

- Will not care as much about your property as you do
- Can be slow to act if the tenant has a problem
- Receives a monthly fee from you that can run anywhere from 7 to 12 percent of the monthly rent you charge
- Often demands an escrow account for fix-up costs
- Often works only with their chosen contractors, which can end up costing you more than if you had done the work yourself or developed your own relationships
- Will indicate hidden costs to you such as additional deposits they require
- Will not seek to control you

Let's say you decide to become a landlord and handle all these issues yourself. The following is a summary of my wisdom on this issue, based on my own experience.

Don't Rent to Friends

Years ago we had friends who were renting in our neighborhood. Their landlord kept raising the rent $50 every six months and eventually they could no longer afford the monthly payment. It just so happened that I had a vacancy coming up on one of my rentals in a neighborhood nearby. This was a perfect solution for them, since their children could continue in the same school district. They stayed on as my tenants for seven years and then finally bought their own house.

When they vacated my property, it was a mess. Not only was everything worn-out, there were holes in the walls and fixtures missing from the ceiling. But what really made me mad was that they had disconnected the washer and dryer (bought from me on a payment plan), and left the hoses leaking water all over the family room. The cost of fixing that alone was more than the original deposit. And the weeds in the yard!

The tenants felt they left the property in good condition. I did not. I refused to give them their deposit back. They got a little nasty as I went around taking pictures of the place in case I needed them in court. We ended up splitting the deposit 50–50. We also split up our friendship. Never rent to friends.

Know the Landlord-Tenant Laws

Get the landlord-tenant laws for your state, county, or city. Know where you stand in advance.

Years ago my son wanted to attend school in New Jersey, where I am originally from. I lease-optioned a property, discounting the rent $200 per month if I paid a year's rent in advance. The owners were moving to Pennsylvania and needed the cash.

One of the conditions of the lease specified that the landlord would have air-conditioning installed by March 31. My lease was due to expire the end of September. But the sellers spent all the advance rent money and had none left over for my air conditioner. Ever been in New Jersey when it's hot and humid? I broke the lease, hired an attorney to recover the rest of my five payments plus my option money. They also hired an attorney. They lost in court. I still have a judgment against the property for money they owe me. Anyone want to buy this judgment? Moral: Know where you stand as a landlord. The courts don't always rule in your favor.

Make Sure Your Lease Protects You

If a tenant breaks the lease before the termination date, the lease they signed should protect you. And of course be sure to screen prospective tenants beforehand. I now do a thorough screening of prospective tenants before they even begin to go through the application process.

I rented a property to a woman from California who had plenty of income to afford the property and passed my screening requirements. She was moving to Colorado and needed a place to live before school started because she had a school-age child. Within four months of leasing the house, she decided she hated Colorado and wanted to move immediately in the dead of the winter back to California. We worked this out, but I have since changed my lease to deal with sudden vacancies in the winter months, when it's impossible to find suitable tenants for your vacant property.

Never Accept Partial Rental Payments

I have a friend who owns a lot of duplexes and four-unit buildings. He let his tenants make partial payments occasionally when money was tight. One month, he needed the full payment from every tenant. He threatened eviction if he did not get paid in full on the first of the month. He ended up in court and lost. The judge ruled that he had set a precedent by accepting partial payments before and thus couldn't enforce his threat when he really needed his money.

Rent for Less

Renting at a discount when the tenants know they're getting a deal gives you a variety of good prospects to choose from. Tenants also tend to stay longer, and this in turn eliminates many of the problems that arise from frequent turnover. Renting for less is a "heads up" signal for tenants to be responsible and timely in their rent payments. This provides justification for you to charge a penalty for late payment.

Rent Control

Rent control limits rent increases, requires payment of fees and charges, tacks on additional costs when tenants move, and restricts sales and conversions without the tenant's approval. There are over 200 cities and counties across the country that have rent control regulations. Supporters of rent control say it is needed to prevent landlords from charging outrageous rents to the elderly, disabled, and poor. Opponents argue that rent control discourages property development, thereby lowering the supply of units and forcing rents up.

Finding Tenants

Most people look for tenants by advertising their properties in the newspaper. Or they might put a "House for Rent" sign in the front yard with their telephone number.

Not me. I don't want prospective tenants calling me. I want them to take the initiative and view the property. I advertise a rental open house, scheduled for only two hours on a Sunday. The ad typically reads like this:

House for Rent

Cute, Cozy and Clean

3 bed/2 bath home in southwest part of town.

Fenced yard, garage, and new paint throughout.

Open Sunday from 1:00–3:00 P.M. $950 disc. rent.

Pets negotiable. 123 East Main Street

Get Started

How to Establish Your Rent

· Property managers and your local newspaper can assist you with research in determining what the fair market rental is in the areas where you own property. Also, check into whether there is a local apartment owners' association or real estate investment association. Attend meetings and become acquainted with their members. Network.

· Keep the economy in mind. Know what is happening where you live and what is projected to happen over the next six months to a year.

· Make sure your leases expire at prime rental times such as June or July if you are renting to families. They will need to relocate before the school year begins.

· Determine exactly who pays what. For example, in my single family house rentals, my tenants pay all utilities. In a mobile home park, however, the owner may end up paying utilities.

· Rent increases protect you against inflation. Decide how you can realistically raise the rent each year. Have a good accountant who understands how depreciation works and your basis in each property. Every dollar lost in rental income causes further loss-of-interest income.

· Be sure to carry adequate insurance and that your tenant has rental insurance.

· Save all receipts for improvements to your rentals and keep good records. Almost anything is deductible, but you must have documentation for the IRS.

Don't Forget

Find out what the rent control regulations are where you live. This will affect your strategy in buying and holding real estate for the long term.

Similarly, consider the fair housing laws where you live and buy property. These are state and federal laws that protect classes of people from housing discrimination. The Federal Fair Housing Act prohibits discrimination on the basis of race, color, religion, sex, national origin, disability, and family status (such as a single mother with seven children). If you own less than three single family homes, this law does not apply, provided you rent and mortgage your properties on your own.

Notice that I do not include a telephone number. I arrive 15 minutes early for the open house, and usually I am greeted by motivated tenants who want to see the property. The mention of "discount rent" is the draw. Mentioning that pets are negotiable also brings out people, because most landlords simply don't allow them. I tell them I have to see the pet first and then decide. All attack-trained animals are excluded, and no tenant may have more than two pets. I charge extra per pet, and that fee and deposit are negotiable.

After the prospective tenants have viewed the property, I have applications ready. There is a $25 nonrefundable deposit for an authorized credit and reference check. Once qualified, I notify the tenant I select and tell the other applicants that the property has been rented. I only cash one $25 check at a time, so I can return the checks to the other prospective tenants who did not get the property.

Open houses have worked well for me in my search for tenants. If I price the property right and allow pets, I usually can get a good selection of qualified tenants.

Quick Tips

Note: If I like any of the other applicants, I will ask them if they would like to remain on a waiting list. Then if I have a vacancy, I call them first. This has worked well for me in the past couple of years. In two cases, tenants who looked at one property and were wait-listed were eventually placed in another.

Screening Tenants for Rentals

Once a prospective tenant completes the rental application, I sit down with them and ask this question: "Is there anything else I need to know before I check your credit?" The answers can range anywhere from "I bounced a check at the supermarket two years ago" to "I filed bankruptcy last week."

My purpose in asking this question is to determine if the tenant is being honest with me. When I pull their credit report, will it match what they tell me themselves? I look for long-term tenants who will take good care of my property. Hence, I do my homework to assure myself that they will follow through with their responsibilities.

Get Started

Putting the wrong tenant in your property could cost you more than dollars. It could cost you many hours of anguish. For this reason it is also important to check landlord and employment references. More than once a former landlord has advised me not to rent to a prospective tenant. The questions you want to ask former landlords are:

• Would you rent to these tenants again?

• What was the condition of the property when they vacated?

• How long did they live there?

• Were they ever late with their rent?

Answers to these questions help you make an informed decision about your prospects.

Don't Forget

If you do not belong to a credit bureau to check out a prospective tenant's credit, you can register with a company that does credit and background checks for a nominal fee. On the Internet, search for "credit checking companies." One Web site is *www.tenantchk.com.*

Signing the Lease

When you (the lessor) and your tenant (the lessee) execute a lease, you both agree to several things, including the expiration date of the lease, the monthly rent, and the rights and privileges of both the tenant and landlord.

Legally speaking, a properly drawn lease is a binding contract for both parties. In most states, the law is in favor of the tenant, so it is important that your lease spell out the responsibilities of both parties and is fair to all concerned. If one area of the lease is ever contested, the rest of the lease should still be valid.

I feel this lease is beneficial both to the landlord and the tenant. Be careful that your lease or any legal document you use has been blessed by an attorney in the state you are investing in, not just the state where you reside. Having your attorney review this document before you use any part of it protects you. Due to different state laws, there may be items that would not be applicable to your state. The following lists the key property management policies that I developed to avoid problems by addressing them early in the leasing process.

- I do my lease signings at a neutral location, such as a coffee shop. I buy the new tenant a cup of coffee, and we take our time going over the provisions step by step.

- I require a cashier's check, certified funds, or cash initially. I accept personal checks after the initial security deposit and first month's rent have been received.

- I have a two-tiered rent system: retail and discount. When I offer a property at a discount, I explain to the tenant that the retail rent is the rent they owe if they are past the discount date. For example, if I rent a property for $950 per month discounted rent, that means the retail rent is $1,000. I am giving them a $50 discount if they pay me by the last business day of the month at 5:00 P.M. If the last business day is Friday, the 28th, and they pay on the 29th, they lost their discount and the rent is then $1,000. However, they are not late on their rent. If they pay after the first of the month, they owe the $1,000 plus a 5 percent late fee. As you can see, it saves the tenant $100 per month to make timely payments.

- No appliances are covered in this contract. I tell the tenant when we conduct the walk-through that we will test all appliances. If something breaks down within the first month, I will replace it. After that, the tenant either has to replace it or fix it at their expense. If they replace an item, they are welcome to take it with them when they leave. I cannot warranty appliances I did not buy, since I do not know their condition or age.

- Make sure you have spaces at the bottom of each page of the lease for both you, the "agent," and the tenant to initial. I don't like to use the term "owner." This way if there is a problem, I can appeal to a "partner" before I answer the issue.

- I ask to meet any pets the tenant wants to live with. If they're okay, I ask the tenant what he or she feels is a fair monthly fee for this privilege. I accept nothing under $25 per pet, limit of two. I also collect extra security for damages. Pets' names and the monthly amount are listed in a pet clause.

- I do not allow subleasing, nor do I accept partial rent payments. Please stay true to this or your lease won't be worth the paper it is written on.

- When terminating the lease, I wait 15 days after the tenant vacates the property and after I verify that all utilities have been paid before releasing the security deposit (if the property was left in the same condition as originally occupied). The reason for the 15 days is that in some cities or counties the government can put a lien against a property for unpaid utilities. If after 15 days the final bill still hasn't been paid, I contact the tenant and tell them I can't release the security deposit until the utilities are taken care of. Why don't I not just take the money out of their security deposit? Because if they did not take care of the place, they won't be getting all or any of their deposit returned. I don't want to be stuck. If the utility company hasn't received final payment after 30 days, I then pay it and the tenants forfeit their deposit.

- I add any additional exceptions or fees in the special provisions clause of the lease. For example, if the tenant needs a washer and dryer but doesn't have the money, I buy the appliances and put them in the property for an additional $25 per month. I had one tenant paying $25 per month for seven years! I have had tenants ask me about cleaning services, lawn care, and trash removal. I put all of these extras and their monthly fees under special provisions.

Property Inspection and Walk-Through

Once the lease is signed and money is in hand, we go to the property for a walk-through. Every item in every room is checked for damage: window treatments, walls, carpet, flooring, toilets, sinks, tiles, gutters, landscaping, and so on.

Once we complete our initial walk-through, I take one copy of the inspection report with me and leave a copy with the tenant. They have an additional three days to make any other notes on this inspection sheet. Three days later I pick up the sheet and we all sign off that the property was inspected and accepted by the tenant. The first copy is destroyed, and the second is the legal one on which the inspection was based. I tell the tenants that this is for their protection so that they're not charged for any damage for which they were not responsible.

Don't Forget

It is very important that you and the new resident go over every inch of the property together and that you note the condition of all items and whether any repairs or replacements are needed.

One of my tenants moved into a property in excellent condition with a beautiful, large backyard. Trees, flowers, and shrubs were all beautiful. Two years later when the tenant left, the yard was ruined. I kept the security to use for getting the yard back to its original condition. Check everything!

I also take pictures before they move in and after they move out. Pictures do speak a thousand words . . . in court.

Other Property Management Issues

Student Rentals

You either love them or hate them. Student rentals offer additional cash flow, since students rent by the room as compared to a family renting one dwelling.

However, you never know what to expect. Will each of the students pay on time? Will they maintain the property? Will they be cited for disturbing the peace at all hours of the night?

As landlords, we are not allowed to discriminate against students. We are, however, allowed to put provisions in the lease that protect the neighborhood and privacy of others.

One landlord I know had one of her children living in a four-bedroom house and rented out the other three rooms at $400 each. She made $200 a month positive cash flow after expenses. Her son lived in the home rent-free and managed the property and the students.

If you have a child in college, this could be a great way to invest in property and make a return. If you decide to rent to students, a good fail-safe is to require their parents to cosign the lease and make them responsible for the rent. In college towns, vacancies are rare. Even in the summer months, incoming students often lease for a full year so they have a guaranteed residence in the fall.

Quick Tips

Infrequent vacancies, decent management in place, and guaranteed payments by the parents make student rentals an investment choice for your portfolio.

Government Rental Programs

I myself have never worked with government programs, but here are details about Section 8 housing.

Funded by HUD and run by the State Housing Authority, Section 8 provides vouchers to individuals and families whose annual income falls in the "extremely low" or "very low" categories according to HUD guidelines. This program was set up so that low-income families could secure decent, safe, and sanitary housing. The tenant contributes 30 percent of his or her monthly income, and the Section 8 program pays the rest. The advantage for the landlord is a guaranteed check from the government each month for 70 percent of the rent. The drawback is whether the tenant will meet that 30 percent obligation. Here are some frequently asked questions:

What type of housing qualifies for Section 8?

Single family homes, apartments, duplexes, and mobile homes. A unit must have one bedroom for every two occupants. It cannot be owner-occupied. The unit must be in good condition and pass HUD's inspection requirements.

How does an owner determine if a family is eligible for Section 8?

Before a family can look for a unit of housing, they must be issued a certificate or voucher stating their eligibility. This also shows the period of time allotted to them to find housing, usually 60 days. If an acceptable unit cannot be found within that time frame, the voucher is given to the next person on the waiting list. (Note: You should contact HUD before making a commitment to a family. The unit must pass inspection, and a lease and contract must be signed before the family moves in and before subsidy payments can begin.)

How is the lease handled?

The local HUD staff prepares the lease and contract between you and the tenant so that payments are authorized to you, the owner.

How much can an owner charge for rent?

Fair market rent is set by HUD. This is based on what is available in the area. The amount of the rent plus utilities cannot exceed the fair market rent.

Does the tenant pay any rent?

Tenants pay no more than 30 percent of their monthly income.

Who pays utilities?

This is negotiated between the landlord and tenant. When possible, the tenant pays; otherwise, the landlord is entitled to charge a higher rent.

Who chooses the tenants?

Screening for desirable tenants is the responsibility of the landlord. HUD determines only whether the tenant is eligible for Section 8 housing.

How often are inspections done?

Inspections are done every 12 months for as long as the unit remains in the program. If the tenant damages a unit or takes action that causes a unit not to pass inspection, it is the owner's responsibility to make any needed repairs or corrections. The owner may bill and/or evict the tenant for tenant damages.

How long is the family eligible for assistance?

A family is certified as eligible for a 12-month period and must be recertified every 12 months on their anniversary date.

May an owner evict a Section 8 tenant?

Yes.

Are rental increases allowed?

An owner can request a rental increase every 12 months at the time of the anniversary date. The amount of the increase is adjusted and controlled by HUD. In addition, the rental increase may only be given if rents other then Section 8 went up in comparable neighborhoods.

When and how does an owner get the rental money each month?

The owner is responsible for collecting the tenant's portion of the rent. This should be collected on the first of each month. An owner can collect late charges, but this must be designated in the lease as an addendum.

How does an owner become a Section 8 landlord?

Contact your local Section 8 staff. This is handled through the state or local government housing office.

Don't Forget

It is imperative to comply with the Federal Housing Act. See www.hud.gov/groups/fairhousing.cfm for more details.

Get Started

Online Resources for Landlords

Check these Web sites for a wealth of information on property management issues:

- www.relibrary.com provides real estate industry news and resources.

- www.landlord.com is a comprehensive site featuring forms, letters, articles, and news.

- www.cses.com/rental offers forms, tax advice, property acquisition, and more.

- www.mv.com/ipusers/nbpoa/other.htm contains landlord/tenant statutes for all 50 states.

- www.nolo.com provides free information about many landlord/tenant issues.

It's a Wrap

✓ Handle problems immediately, before they escalate.

✓ Determine whether or not to manage the property yourself.

✓ Establish the right rent for you and sustain a positive cash flow.

✓ Screen potential tenants carefully.

✓ Conduct a property walk-through once the lease is signed.

✓ Use Web sites for helpful information.

Capturing Profit from Your Investments

Do I Need to Read This Chapter?

➜ You don't know when to sell your property.

➜ You don't know how to sell your property.

➜ You want to prepare a property for selling.

➜ What are the tax benefits of property exchanges?

Selling Your Property

Eventually, you will want or need to sell your investment property. The reasons may arise from issues in your personal life, but more often there are compelling reasons to sell from a business standpoint:

- Profit! Your property has appreciated significantly in value, and you decide to capture your profit.

- Changes in your financial goals or business circumstances.

- Loss of depreciation benefits.

- Increased equity, so you can pyramid your initial investment into a larger investment. Owning a property is a forced savings plan. With this savings, you can take money out of a property in the form of a second mortgage or home equity loan and use that as a down payment for another property. This is pyramiding your initial investment. However, if you are the type of person who dislikes being constantly financially encumbered, this type of leveraging strategy may not be advisable for you.

- Incurable problems, such as a deteriorating neighborhood, major expenses that cannot be profitably absorbed, or continuous negative cash flow.

An easy and advantageous way to sell your property is to convert a tenant to a buyer. That way you pay no realtor commissions or points, and your buyer is already in place. If your tenant has always been timely with rent and wants to buy your property, you benefit from his demonstrated commitment to the neighborhood and the fact that he will take good care of your property as a future owner. Committed tenants have time to save for a down payment as well as to arrange for financing.

In most cases, however, you will have to find a buyer. Before going public, try networking among other professionals who have an interest in real estate, such as insurance agents, other investors, property managers, and realtors. Prepare a detailed information sheet on the property for distribution. Word of month works wonders.

If this method brings no immediate prospects, it's time to market to the public:

- Put a "For Sale" sign in front of the property. The National Association of Realtors claims that over 70 percent of all property sales arise from yard signs.

- Advertise in the classifieds with a "Rent to Own" or "Lease with Option to Buy" ad. It's wise not to include the property address in your ad, to avoid a parade of "lookie lou's." Mention such things as low down payment or excellent terms, but only state the price. That and your phone number are the only numbers that should appear. When a prospect calls for information, you can determine whether he is serious or just a "tire kicker."

- Include all selling points in your ad. Provide enough detail to motivate a prospect to pick up the phone to inquire and make an appointment. Use features such as:

  - Great location—close to schools, shopping, public transportation
  - Excellent neighborhood—quiet, secluded, nice area
  - Attractive, well-built, remodeled, etc.
  - Extra features, extra large closets, laundry room, dishwasher, etc.
  - Quality tenants and excellent rental history
  - Tax shelter possibilities and excellent return on investment

- Schedule an open house.

Preparing Your Property for Viewing

First impressions count, so consider curb appeal. Trim all trees and shrubs and make all landscaping look presentable. Install large house numbers on the front of the home, and consider installing a decorative front door or refinishing the existing door. Make sure the exterior paint looks fresh.

Inside, do a thorough cleaning, and repaint with light, neutral colors. Replace smoke detectors or install new batteries in them. Allot the majority of your fix-up budget to the kitchen and bathrooms. In the kitchen, clean all appliances and make sure the sink is not marred. If appliances need to be replaced, buy good used ones or put an allowance in for the purchaser. Consider putting new hardware on cabinetry. In the bathrooms, install fresh shower curtains or thoroughly clean shower doors. Replace outdated faucets. Refinish the tub or shower and sink, if needed. Clean the ceiling and wall fixtures. In the bedrooms, replace ceiling light fixtures with fans. Install inexpensive but fresh-looking window treatments.

Don't Forget

 Be careful not to overspend. Your goal is to make the property clean, fresh, and livable. Make it tasteful and neutral. If flooring needs replacement, install neutral linoleum or hardwood flooring.

1031 Exchanges

This is the exchange of one investment property type for another with no tax consequence. The IRS looks at an exchange as if you were extending your first investment onto the next property as it increases in value.

Say you buy a duplex for $100,000, which has a $60,000 loan against it with $40,000 in equity. If you trade that duplex for a triplex costing $200,000, you are trading your equity into a new property. As long as you keep extending your investment and the price goes up, there is no tax consequence. But if you make the exchange and have to put in additional assets, or "boot" to make the payment (for example, cash, rare coins, jewelry, cars, anything of value that is not considered like-kind property), that is considered added cash, which means a tax consequence.

Types of 1031 Exchanges

The following types of exchanges are available:

Direct Exchange

Two parties agree to exchange a property. This is very rare.

Three-Party Exchange

Three transactions are part of one closing:

- An owner who wishes to sell but also wishes to own another property.
- A buyer who wishes to buy the seller's property.
- An owner of a property that the first party wants to buy.

Delayed Exchange

Also known as a "Starker exchange," it allows an owner to sell a property and have the proceeds held in escrow for a property not yet chosen. The seller cannot have control of the funds. The seller must identify the property he or she wishes to buy within 45 days and purchase it within 180 days of the original closing.

Reverse Exchange

A buyer locates a property to buy before selling a currently owned property. In this case, an intermediary buys the replacement property, using funds provided by you before you sell the existing property. The intermediary holds the replacement property until you sell, then transfers the title to you as part of a 1031 tax-deferred exchange. Hire an intermediary with experience for this transaction, because this type of exchange is complicated.

Three requirements that qualify you for an exchange:

- The property you are acquiring is larger than the one you are giving.
- You are acquiring extra indebtedness.
- You receive no cash or boot in the transaction. (Boot is something of value in lieu of cash, such as a boat or a car.)

Steps in an Exchange

- Identify the property you intend to "buy" in the exchange within 45 days of the closing on your property.
- Close on the second property within 180 days of the previous closing or by the due date of your taxes in the year of the sale of your property, whichever occurs first.

- An intermediary or a party outside of your control must be the escrow for the exchange.

It's a Wrap

✓ Know when the time is right to sell and act on it.

✓ Prepare your property to get the highest selling price you can.

✓ Advertise what you're selling to attract the right buyers.

✓ Look into property exchanges for potential tax benefits.

CHAPTER 10

Writing a Business Plan for Real Estate Investors

Do I Need to Read This Chapter?

➡ You don't know how to create an effective business plan.

➡ You don't know why you even need a business plan.

➡ You plan to borrow money to finance your business.

➡ You don't know where to get help with your plan.

Having a business plan is different from having a marketing plan. A marketing plan is the vehicle that helps you generate leads and promotes your business. A business plan is an overall picture of the business from marketing to its financial health, including what the organization looks like in terms of its employees and businesses. Let's look at a few solid reasons why business plans are the backbone of successful companies, from the independent owner to the Fortune 500 companies.

The Importance of Business Plans

Researchers have found that small companies that have a business plan have not only survived in their business, but have had successful growth every year since the inception of their business plans.

Quick Tips

According to an AT&T survey, only 42 percent of all businesses actually have a business plan. A plan demonstrates commitment on your part to make the dream for the business a reality.

If you're thinking about borrowing any money to fund your business, or are looking for private investment, a business plan is a must. I know of no one in the real estate business who uses credit lines or private money and does not have a plan.

You are perceived as a successful business person when you can walk into a bank, or the Small Business Administration office, with a plan about your business and how you will expand it. Without a business plan, no one in the financial world will take you seriously.

A business plan helps to organize the details of your company, its goals, and the steps management will take to make the goals happen. It is easier to anticipate changes and plan for them on paper than to adjust to business changes in real life.

Planning Your Plan

Consider these questions before you begin writing your business plan:

1. How much do you know about the industry?

2. Have you looked at other business plans? (If not, you can find a sample business plan in Appendix A.)

3. Are you willing to put the time and effort into constructing and using a business plan?

4. Are you open to creative ways of doing things and making new opportunities?

5. Do you currently have a plan? Has it ever been updated?

Get Started

 Six Steps to Writing a Good Business Plan

1. Set aside enough quiet time. This can't be done in one hour. Spend sufficient time.

2. Determine in advance what you want to accomplish with your plan. Are you preparing a plan that will help you borrow money, recruit investors, or map out a new venture?

3. Research additional topics that you cannot answer.

4. Complete a first draft. Review it for accuracy.

5. Have the draft reviewed by a professional. Ask for advice and get opinions.

6. Complete the final product and use it!

A good business plan cannot guarantee success, but you can bet that not having one increases your chances of failing. If you don't know where you're going, you probably won't ever get there.

Business Plan Outline

Let's look at a business plan outline and what needs to be addressed to make the plan work. Each of these headings should be on a separate page.

1. *Title page.* Include the name of your business, address, phone number, and the names of the owners.

2. *Table of contents.* This allows the reader to quickly find what they're looking for without reading the entire document.

3. *Executive summary.* The summary is often the only section potential investors read. Do not make it longer than two pages. Among the points that should be covered are:

- Current status of your business, when the business started or is expected to start.

- Description of what your business does.

- Information about the market and your plan for reaching it.

- Your unique way of achieving your marketing objectives, including marketplace strengths.

- Long-term and short-term plans.

- Financial projections.

- If you're trying to borrow money, the amount you need and how you will use it.

4. *Business and industry descriptions.* Describe what the business does, standard industry operations, and recent or projected changes in the industry. Let an outsider know how your unique industry operates.

5. *Organizational data.* Outline the duties and responsibilities of all those involved.

6. *Marketing strategy.* Identify your customers, your market, and how you will reach them. Be sure to define:

- Who the customer is

- Total market size

- How you reach your market

- Why your services are needed

- Your unique niche

7. *Competitive analysis.* Identify key players in your area and describe how your business can compete or coexist with theirs.

8. *Financial information.* Illustrate the overall financial condition of your business. If you are an existing business, include these standard financial statements:

- Income statement

- Balance sheet

- Cash-flow statement

9. *Projections.* Include a one-year and three-to-five-year projection covering the future financial picture of the business. Highlight expected revenue, expenses, assets, and liabilities.

Don't Forget

If you want to borrow money, lenders review your plan for certain items, such as:

- How will you be able to pay them back?

- What will you do with the money?

- Why do you need money?

- Does an influx of cash and its proposed use make sense to the business?

- What growth potential is there in the industry?

Even if you do not plan to borrow money immediately, you must plan for the future growth of your company. Chart a course for your company on paper that illustrates how you will take its existing asset base and invest it for the future. If you suddenly decide to borrow some money or it is offered to you at such a relatively low cost that you cannot refuse, it will be too late to dream up a realistic business plan on short notice. Develop your plan now and store it in your computer. Update it in the future by just typing a few words as necessary.

Quick Tips

If you want more assistance on business plan writing, check your local library for books on business plans. There are also software programs that create business plans. Two of the more popular ones are Biz Plan Builder (800–346–5426) and Multi Media MBA (800–228–5609).

Finally, it's not the plan you write that works, it's the implementation. All the plans written in the world make no difference if you don't go out there and work them! Grow your real estate business to new heights with the right plan!

The financial information as well as the projections of the business are important to those who are considering whether to invest any money in your company. You need to show them, or yourself, how you would make your assets grow.

✓ A business plan is a must if you intend to borrow money.

✓ A plan will organize all the details of your company and hopes for it.

✓ Include one-year and three-to-five-year projections.

✓ Have your plan reviewed by a professional.

✓ Get help if you need it.

CHAPTER 11

A Working Marketing Plan for Your Real Estate Business

Do I Need to Read This Chapter?

➔ You don't know why a marketing plan is necessary.

➔ You don't know what should be included in your marketing plan.

➔ You would like to know how to measure your progress against a written plan.

Why a Plan Is Necessary

The most successful people in real estate have a marketing plan. Why?

- The plan helps keep them focused.
- They can evaluate their progress at any time and see if they are on track.
- A good plan acts like a road map. It keeps them going in the direction of their goals.
- If something isn't working, the plan can be changed at any time to meet their needs.

Quick Tips

At a convention I spoke at recently, I asked, "How many of you have a goal for your business?" About half of the audience raised their hands. I then asked, "How many of you have them written down?" About a third of the half kept their hands up. That third is the group of people that I feel have the best chance of growing a successful business.

Most people are afraid to put a plan together? Why?

- They don't know what should be in the plan.

- People are afraid to commit themselves to the actions needed for the plan to be fulfilled.

- Some of us just don't feel like it. It takes work!

Marketing Plan Outline

I have tried to alleviate the difficulties of what to put in a plan by breaking down what should be outlined in a marketing plan. I have also included a sample plan in Appendix B that you can use as a model. Items number 2 and 3 below and in Appendix B—marketing and budget—are up to you. If you are committed to making a go of your business, you need a plan of action to help you get started, stay on track, and modify your actions to achieve success.

I had a boss once who always said you should plan your work, then work your plan.

Goal Setting

Let's start with goal setting for your real estate business. Depending on where you are, your goals need to be realistic and attainable. For instance, if you are new to the business, I'm not sure that a goal of $500,000 a year within the next three months is realistic. What would be attainable, depending on a few other factors that I will outline in the plan, is a goal of closing your first real estate transaction in three months. Many people want to set higher expectations. I prefer the more conservative approach to real estate investing.

Get Started

Start with your goal. Write down what you want to set for yourself as an attainable goal for your business. You cannot do a marketing plan without having the goal first. Take the time, evaluate what you've done with your real estate so far, and set a smart goal!

Laying the Groundwork

A solid marketing plan lays groundwork. Your plan should serve as a foundation for marketing that answers these questions.

1. Who is the targeted audience that you are trying to market?

2. How will you go about marketing to that particular audience?

3. What budget do you have? What is the expected dollars spent compared to the deals closed? Are you netting any money?

4. Who is your competition?

5. Are you an effective time manager? If not, how can you quickly become one?

6. What kind of marketing research is at your disposal?

Don't Forget

It is important that your marketing plan be you. It does not need to be complicated. Save complications for your business plan (see the special report on business plans in Appnedix A). A marketing plan is a subset of a business plan. It is a guide to help you achieve the objectives so you can meet your goal.

Details of the Plan

Let's go through each area of a marketing plan. Start answering these questions as you read through the topics. Examples of how to answer each one are appended.

1. Target Market

Who is my targeted market? This means: Who is my customer? It could be real estate agents, attorneys, CPAs, financial planners, or any other professionals who have clients with a need to sell their home for whatever reason.

2. Marketing Strategy

How will I go about marketing to the audience I am trying to target? If your audience is property sellers, for instance, you could use:

- Direct mail
- Telemarketing
- Advertisements in weekly newspapers
- Articles you write for local newspapers on the benefits and risks of real estate as an investment

If you were to target real estate agents, you could:

- Join the local Board of Realtors and attend their meetings.
- Advertise in the Board of Realtors publications.
- Visit open houses on the weekends to meet real estate agents one on one.

3. Budget

It is important to have an idea of how much money you are going to spend to promote your real estate business. Some expenses to take into consideration are:

- Business cards
- Advertising
- Marketing pieces, flyers, postcards, brochures, letters
- Any list you buy for direct mail or telemarketing
- Direct mail postage and bulk mail permits
- Membership fees in organizations you join that will help generate business
- Dues for professional skills improvement, such as Toastmasters or Dale Carnegie

4. Your Competition

There are people who say they are real estate investors, and there are the quiet ones who are really doing the business. You need to be able to determine who these people are, as well as figure out what they're doing to generate leads.

5. Time Management

Let's start with this question: "How much time do I realistically have to devote to my business?"

This is difficult to answer if you have another job and are fitting real estate into your life with your other activities. You must put down in writing the hours per week and the exact times that you have to devote to marketing.

This question should not just be written down, but pondered based on who you are: What can I do with the time that I have to be the most effective in my marketing?

Some people are good writers, so the marketing they do would be advertising, letter writing, and authoring articles. Some people are good speakers, so they may get out in their communities and network with the professionals in their town. It doesn't matter which you do, but do what appeals to your strength. An introverted person might not enjoy a function at a local restaurant that is arranged for the sole purpose of meeting potential business contacts.

6. Market Research

If you decide to pay for advertising, you should review the following issues:

Cost. The longer the ad runs, the less your cost per issue. Lengthy advertising terms still carry a high overall cost. Always ask for a discount for your advertising.

Type of publication. Is it the local papers you want to be in? Advertise in the weekly papers, ethnic papers, university papers, military papers, or professional publications to set yourself apart from other buyers. Take advantage of any bond you have with a specific type of publication. If you speak a language other than English, make sure to note that in the non-English paper.

Farming. Pick four communities and get to know them. Meet the neighbors, knock on doors, learn the real value, not just the Fair Market Value (FMV).

Don't Forget

If you put your plan together using these six topics as a base for your marketing activity, you'll have a solid foundation to use as a road map for your real estate investment business.

Evaluation

There is still one other thing you must do to be sure your plan is working for you. You must evaluate how you are doing. Here's a checklist of evaluation questions to help you review your progress.

Once-a-week checklist:

1. How many contacts or conversations did I try to initiate this week with my targeted audience?

2. How many times this week did I contact people I know to assist me in building referrals?

3. How much time have I invested this week in promoting my business?

4. Which of my marketing methods produces any business?

Once a month checklist:

1. How many contacts have I made who can help generate business?

2. What type of follow-up have I done with the contact?

3. What new ideas did I implement in growing my business?

4. What marketing pieces am I using that are working? Why are they working?

5. What else could I be doing to enhance my business?

These questions should help keep you on track. Whatever you do, be proactive in marketing your business on a daily basis. Our industry is constantly changing. You need to be involved and current in your marketing to stay ahead of your competition.

Ask yourself every day what you are doing today to work toward your goal.

Don't Forget

Marketing is essential to the survival and growth of your business. Without it you won't make dime one. Have goals. Set realistic objectives. Make a plan. Answer the questions that are outlined for your use. Use the sample marketing plan in Appendix B as your guide. If you follow a plan and evaluate your progress, you can't help but increase your bottom line. And let's face it! Isn't that why you're reading this? Generate more leads and grow your business.

Make a plan and use it!

It's a Wrap

✓ A good marketing plan will help keep you on track to succeed.

✓ Start with your goal—an attainable goal will help you create an actionable plan.

✓ Create an outline—fill it in to reflect how you can best achieve your goal.

✓ Include once-a-week and once-a-month checklists to stay on track.

✓ Stay proactive and use your plan!

CHAPTER 12

Steps for Succeeding in Real Estate

Do I Need to Read This Chapter?

➡ You want to get serious about real estate investing.

➡ You want a realistic four-week plan to get started.

➡ You want to set up your business to succeed.

We covered a huge amount of material in this manual. As I promised you at the beginning, this book aims to familiarize you with everything—soup to nuts—that you need to know to succeed in real estate investing. Naturally, it takes time to become experienced in all of the principles outlined in this book. But as you work, use the summary below as an overview of all you've learned. Refer to it periodically to keep you on target and focused on your goals. These are the highlights of the material that we've covered:

1. Know why you need to invest in real estate.

   a. Establish in your own mind the reasons why you need to invest in real estate in order to stay ahead of taxes and inflation.

   b. Never forget your purchase. Appreciation, cash flow, income, or immediate profits, whichever way you choose.

2. Establish your investment goals.

   a. Prepare a current financial statement estimating major expenditures, where you stand today, and what you face in the future.

   b. Determine how much money you think you need to maintain your present standard of living after you retire.

   c. Allow for inflation. Remember, in a real estate investment, inflation works for you instead of against you.

3. Locate sources of investment capital.

   a. Consider such sources of start-up capital as savings accounts, cash-value life insurance, borrowing against stock, and refinancing of other real estate.

   b. Consider borrowing from people you know who would like to earn a higher interest than on their present investment and still have security.

   c. Don't overleverage. You do not want to be in a position where you feed your investment to keep it running, unless you are prepared to take that risk. If you did a no-money-down deal on a $100,000 property, and the market depreciates 3 percent, instead of an infinite gain, you have an infinite loss.

   d. A property can be optioned if you have enough investment capital available in a short period of time to exercise the option and purchase the building.

   e. An owner who is very motivated to sell may be willing to consider a lease-option, lease-purchase, or outright sale with no money down.

   f. Purchasing a distressed property can be very profitable if you are willing to work at it and get it turned around into a profitable investment.

   g. Enlarge your investment holdings as your capital increases.

4. Determine how involved you'll be in managing your property.

5. Select the investment that's right for you.

6. Determine the form of ownership.

7. Locate your investment property.

8. Analyze your prospective investment.

   a. Can the rents be increased soon after you purchase the property?

   b. Are there any excessive expenses that you can lower?

   c. What alternative financing strategies are available on this property?

   d. What are the overall benefits of owning this particular real estate?

   e. Does the price make sense for this property?

9. Use the financing technique that gives you the best result.

10. Consider the tax consequences.

11. Negotiate the purchase. Lock up the property by making sure that both parties have fully executed the contract, including initialing any changes that are made after the fact.

12. Take the necessary steps before and after the closing

    a. Prepare an estimate closing statement, so you know how much cash you need to close.

    b. Employ a title company or an attorney to do the closing for you.

    c. Make a list of the items you expect to receive from the seller at closing. This includes keys, garage door openers, original leases, any service contract related to the property, etc.

    d. Have the utilities changed over to your name.

    e. Do a final walk-through before closing, and visit the property right after the closing. Meet any tenants that still live on the property.

13. Set up a good record-keeping system

14. Develop a lease that serves your purpose and is fair for the tenant

15. Monitor your investment with a return in mind. Don't fall in love with your investment. If it is not meeting your investment return, sell it.

16. Structure the sale to suit your needs

    a. Establish a reasonable selling price based on actual market value.

    b. Look at the pros and cons of listing your property with a realtor.

    c. If you decide to sell the property yourself, develop attractive ads for the property.

    d. When structuring the sale, remember that taking back secondary financing reduces your cash available for reinvestment.

    e. Consider the tax consequences and whether you can defer any capital gains by exchanging.

17. Secure your financial future

    a. Plan on building your real estate investment portfolio to build your estate.

    b. Do not go into real estate investing expecting to become a millionaire in 12 months. Your goal is to acquire sound investments and let appreciation take over.

    c. Remember that any property leveraged at 100 percent will probably be at a break-even or below. It is important to realize that one vacancy will no doubt take money out of your pocket to keep that investment going.

18. Talk to real estate players. As a beginning investor, you should talk to everyone you meet—brokers, appraisers, tenants, other landlords—to get a feel for your individual marketplace. Real estate is a competitive business, but I have found that many of the players are more than happy to talk about their deals once they are completed. Attend and become a part of your local real estate investment club.

Get Started

Your Action Plan

Outlining an action plan based on my experience is easy. I can tell you how to get started, how to stay on track, and how to modify your action plan. But the actual commitment is up to you.

Psychologists say that if you can stick with a plan for four weeks or more, you can maintain your commitment. Like exercising, the first two weeks may be tough, but once you've been committed for those four weeks, you are most likely to be successful.

Because I can't be there personally to cheer you on, you have to want this to happen. With that in mind, here's my outline of a four-week plan that you can focus on to develop your business.

Week 1: Get Organized

Read this entire book once. Then go back and read the comments again. Write down your reasons for investing and what your ultimate goals are. Be as specific as you can. How much time can you reasonably expect to spend doing the work? Will you have someone like a spouse working in a supportive role?

Set up your business administratively. Order business cards. Set up your communication lines, such as a computer and Internet connection, voice mail for your telephone, fax machine, post office box, etc.

Open a bank account for your business. Buy local business insurance and inquire about an umbrella policy that protects you over and above homeowner limits.

Week 2: Check Out the Market

Study the local classifieds and real estate ads, both for sale and for rent information. What's out there? What are the economics of your market? Visit a few open houses on the weekend in areas where you want to invest. Talk to the realtors as well as to the owners selling their property themselves. Learn how they operate. Think about how you would begin the art of negotiation by listening and learning from those who are motivated to sell.

Quick Tips

Research the courthouse if you're doing foreclosures, or the Internet for both foreclosures and for finding deals.

Learn the rental market. What are properties renting for in your "farm" area? Call property managers. Check the Internet to determine market rents.

Start developing relationships with local banks and mortgage companies. Find out what amount of financing you qualify for and how many rentals you can tie up conventionally. Ask what kind of paperwork they need from you and get it to them. It's a good feeling to know that you have some financing in place. If you are not eligible for any financing, look into home equity lines of credit.

Week 3: Go Shopping!

It's time to find those deals! Visit a couple of real estate offices. Explain that you're a real estate investor and are looking for property. Ask for comps in your "farm" areas. Believe me, real estate agents will bend over backward if they think you are a source of commission.

Start driving around and looking at properties for sale. Call the seller or the agent and get some information about the property to see if it qualifies with what you're trying to do.

Track the details of properties you've seen, decide on whether they should be pursued, and decide what your next step should be.

Week 4: Let the Negotiations Begin

Evaluate the fairness of the asking price of a property and make an offer. Remember: The asking price is just that; it's a starting point. If uncertain, go back through the negotiation section of this book and review the questions about motivation. Put those questions to an actual seller. You just never know how motivated someone is until you make an offer.

Have your contracts ready if you're working with an FSBO. If you're working with a realtor, or if the property is listed with a realtor, you will probably use a standard real estate contract. Never check the "specific performance" box, which makes you liable to go through with the purchase, and make sure you have contingencies in place to protect you before you sign anything.

Get your financing together. If interest rates are low, lock in. You usually have a 30- to 60-day lock-in period, which means the deal has to close by then or you lose the rate.

Don't Forget

Get a prequalified letter from your lender or mortgage broker that says you qualify for the amount you think you will need. This is as impressive as cash to a seller when he reads it. This is especially important if you're just starting out, since this will give you credibility and confidence.

Week 5: You're Off and Running!

By now you are repeating the work in week two, three, and four continually. Keep looking for deals. As a property goes under contract, stay on top with your due diligence. Did the property appraise? How did the home inspection go? How are you taking title to the property? Did the title come back clear? Will closing take place with a title company or with an attorney?

Get an exact amount from the realtor or attorney as to what you need to bring to closing in certified funds.

Know exactly what you're going to do with this property after closing. Are you keeping it for rental? Are you holding it for just a couple of years? If you are flipping, you hopefully have found a buyer. Doing the due diligence here is just as important, since your profit will come at closing.

Don't Forget

When you know what happens next, you will always be prepared in case of last minute contingencies or changes. And nine times out of 10, there will be last minute changes!

I stated I was giving you a four-week plan. Obviously, the first week is business startup and won't be repeated. Weeks two through five are the real core of my four-week plan. The tasks in those four weeks are ongoing. You must always be working your business.

Quick Tips

You will likely make offers on many properties that won't be accepted, but don't give up. Keep looking for opportunities and do your homework. Make offers, negotiate, be prepared to walk away at times, and eventually a good deal will come your way. This is not a get-rich-quick business, but steady and profitable over the long term.

✓ An action plan can help you get started and stay on track.

✓ Research the market thoroughly.

✓ Go shopping!

✓ Know in advance what your plans are for your new property.

✓ Don't give up.

Appendix A

Sample Business Plan

ABC Investments
123 East Main Street
Anytown, USA 12345
(123)456–7890

John and Jane Doe
Owners

The Business Plan of ABC Investments

Table of Contents

Competitive Analysis

Financial Information

Projections

Executive Summary

About the company

ABC Investments, a sole proprietorship, was founded by John and Jane Doe in 1993. The company is housed in Houston, Texas. John is the president, and Jane is vice president. Their business is the buying and selling of residential real estate in Texas.

About the industry

There has been a substantial increase in the number of investors diversifying into real estate notes and mortgages. To stay ahead of the competition, John and Jane have recently added structured settlements and annuities to their real estate investment business.

About their individual marketplace

ABC has a detailed marketing plan in place. The plan talks specifically about how they will generate leads. Their main plan for reaching this market is through third-party sources. Both John and Jane are well connected in their community and have developed a referral system in working with professionals and their clients who help bring potential transactions to ABC investments.

Unique selling advantage for ABC

Jane is involved with her local real estate investor association, Real Estate Investors Club of Houston (RICH). She has developed a networking group of experienced investors. Thanks to her connections, Jane is in the unique position of being an educated investor. She has learned creative ways of finding sound investment properties for her portfolio.

Long-term and short-term goals

With a firm foundation in place, ABC has acquired 24 properties in their portfolio since its inception in 1993. ABC's short-term goal is to bring in an additional support person to help John and Jane manage their portfolio of properties so that more time can be spent on finding higher-end properties for their portfolio. ABC's long-term goal is to own 24 properties free and clear at $300,000 each.

Financial projections

Starting out with a $50,000 investment in 1993, ABC has grown to over $450,000 of net revenue primarily from buying and selling real estate. Expected projections in the next three years are to exceed $1 million in assets, with a 15 to 20% growth spurt in real estate.

Financial information

ABC is looking for a line a credit of $500,000. The credit line would be used to secure larger quarters for the company. Adding an additional employee as well as additional equipment, such as a computer, telephone, desk, and other materials, is necessary.

A $100,000 loan is needed now. The company would like to have a credit line established so that money will not be an obstacle when they are ready to expand their business. A repayment plan can be structured for a pay-off over three years, with a possible two-year renewable term.

Business and Industry Description

ABC Investments is an active investor in the real estate and paper industry. Besides acquiring real estate, they are involved in the following:

- Brokering of discounted mortgages
- Representatives of institutional investors in real estate and insurance paper

The most profitable aspect of ABC Investments is using their contacts and their time to find and negotiate real estate–related transactions.

Since interest rates have been down, the company has refinanced their real estate. This has helped grow ABC, since they wholesale about 20% of the real estate transactions they close.

ABC wants to continue to build their real estate portfolio and grow their properties until they come up with the right mix of real estate and private mortgages for their portfolio.

Organizational Data

Founded in 1993, ABC Investments is led by:

John Doe — President

Jane Doe — Vice President of Marketing

John is primarily responsible for running the business from an administrative and financial perspective. He is very involved in the community as a city council member.

John is well known as a buyer of real estate. He has worked with professionals who have clients who need to sell their real estate quick for cash.

Jane is very well connected in the insurance industry. She has brokered in excess of $1 million in annuities and structured settlements to two main investors who specialize in that paper. She enjoys the paper industry and sees brokering paper as a profit center.

Marketing Strategy

The marketing strategy is divided into three areas:

- Real estate buy and hold
- Real estate rehabs and flipping property for profit
- Paper brokering

Real Estate

The real estate area is growing, especially in new construction. John will add builders and developers to the list of other professionals he solicits.

The majority of the marketing is done in Texas, since this is a state where they live in. The creation of seller financing in all three areas is on the rise, with a total market growth expected to be over 20% in each of the next two years. Rehab and flipping of properties is growing in excess of 25% per year.

The best ways ABC can promote their business is by:

- Direct marketing to prospects through direct mail and telemarketing.
- Making presentations and offering training through the Board of Realtors, working community functions, and speaking at events that are financially related. John does most of this.
- Advertising in the weekly, senior, and university papers. Jane tracks and tests ads for leads generated from all advertising.
- Online by chatting and helping in real estate forums.

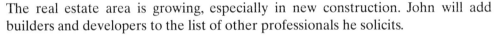

Being a keynote speaker at the local RICH club.

Insurance Paper

By understanding and being involved in the paper industry, Jane promotes her business by writing articles for the publications their referral sources read.

Competitive Analysis

There is competition in the Houston market for real estate, but not outside a radius of approximately 100 miles. ABC combines advertising using multiple county and affiliated publishers in all the weekly newspapers throughout the state. They avoid the metropolitan Houston papers due to heavy competition. Also, none of the competition advertises in the senior or university papers, which bring leads to ABC.

There are two key players in Houston. One is PRIVA, specializing in high-end property. The average property PRIVA purchases is $250,000. ABC buys real estate on a smaller scale, normally in the $150,000 range. When ABC does run across a deal that large, they refer it through PRIVA, which helps maintain good relationships. ABC would like to expand their business to compete with PRIVA.

The other key player in Houston is a newcomer. Abe Faye has been in the real estate business nine years, but recently relocated to Houston. A private investor, he advertises heavily. ABC has talked with Abe about working together. Abe speaks on the national circuit and is very well known in the industry.

ABC feels that they can maintain their business easily, but they have a desire to grow. There is plenty of room for competitors, according to John. ABC wants to enlist and even recruit Abe in their new business venture.

Financial Information

ABC Investments is looking for a line of credit for $500,000. A $100,000 loan is needed to secure larger quarters and buy the equipment needed for a new employee, whom they hope to hire over the next 30 days.

A repayment schedule over three years would be sufficient for the $100,000 loan. An additional two-year renewable term would be an adequate cushion for any expected emergencies or buying opportunities. They can pay off the debt with the existing payments they receive monthly from their portfolio.

ABC can put up collateral for the $500,000 line in the form of notes and real estate.

Since the beginning of their business, they have been profitable every year, as the attached statements reflect. They have not moved since they opened their offices. With an additional person coming on board, they need more space.

[Note: No balance sheet or income statement was generated for this Special Report sample.]

Projections

One-Year Projection

Our projection for the next fiscal year is to grow the business a minimum of 10% or $15,000 net after salaries, expenses, and marketing costs are absorbed.

Three-Year Projection

Our three-year projection is to gross $3 million for a net revenue of $250,000 per year.

Five-Year Projection

Our five-year projection is to gross $6 million, with a net revenue of $500,000 per year.

Appendix B

Sample Marketing Plan

Sample Marketing Plan

    for

Your Company, Inc.

Date

The Goal

To be able to buy a minimum of 16 properties in calendar year 2006, six to keep, and 10 to flip for a net revenue of $180,000 after all marketing and administrative costs. This represents a net growth of 20% over last year's volume.

1. The Customer

Our primary customers are sellers of higher property or professional referral sources I have met over the last few years. They include real estate agents, attorneys, financial planners, CPAs, builders, and developers.

We are developing new contacts to help generate and increase our customer base. These include commercial real estate brokers and leasing agents. We are experimenting with ways to reach private real estate investors to see if they want to be a part of our network.

2. Target Marketing

Existing Markets

For real estate agents, I will continue to be involved in the local Board of Realtors by attending meetings and writing articles for the monthly publication. I will also utilize the sold book information on property analysis that I get from my membership as an affiliate member of my local board.

Attorneys and financial-planner contacts can be fostered through the after-hour Chamber of Commerce functions, Rotary, and other civic organizations, as well as ads in their quarterly publications.

New Markets

I have done a mailing. Commercial real estate broker and leasing agent contacts have been a tremendous benefit. Having been endorsed by the largest commercial real estate company in town, I am getting ready to attend a conference by invitation-only to lenders on commercial real estate.

We joined the local real estate investment group in my area, and I have been invited to the landlord association and exchanger meetings. I plan on bringing information to leave on their community table. I expect to network with these people. I will also be speaking next month to one of the largest real estate investment groups in the country, where I expect attendance to be between 300 to 500 people.

3. Budget

The cost of real estate, builder, and developer connections is $1,500 per year in the form of membership and research fees. Article writing is free PR. I have closed six transactions that I can attribute to these markets.

Attorney and financial planner ads run $750 per year. Since this is new advertising for us, I have yet to see what we got from this venue. The Chamber of Commerce dues cost $300 per year and are well worth every cent in contacts. Even those outside of my targeted audiences have brought me business.

New Markets

We incurred the following costs to date:

Commercial real estate brokers and leasing agents $1,400

Real estate investment club 175

Speaking engagements 0

Marketing pieces for all markets 500

Total costs to date 2,000

Expected costs through year end 2,000

Total budget projection 4,000

Profit on xx transactions closed $210,000

4. Competition

I have found only one true competitor in my area. Mr. Smith has been a real estate investor as well as a loan origination business for over 20 years. He rarely is ever in my targeted markets. Occasionally, we quote on the same deal found by different sources. I have befriended Mr. Smith and have used him as a money source on deals that were unconventional in nature.

5. Time Management

I spend approximately 40 hours per week marketing. Another 10 hours per week is spent on administrative work. I limit the miscellaneous remainder to 10 hours for a total of 60 hours per week. Only six of those hours come on weekends.

I devote a third of my marketing time to building a referral-based business and meeting new people who can help generate leads for me. I spend another quarter of my time on direct mail and other direct mailing methods. I spend the balance of the marketing time making presentations to my targeted audiences.

6. Market Research

I am researching legal papers for direct mail to estate and bankruptcy attorneys. I have run ads in attorney and CPA quarterly publications and am testing for results. There is nothing to report at this early date. I am researching a presentation that will dovetail real estate investing with the note business so that I can present it to real estate investors around the country.

I want to attend paper and real estate–related conventions next year as a speaker as well as an attendee for further continuing education. Investor contacts have given me numbers to call, and I will attend at least two meetings before offering my services as a speaker.

I will evaluate my progress weekly and will sit down to make modifications to my marketing plan if needed next quarter.

Addendum to Last Quarter

Our original projection to grow our business a minimum of 10% this year was achieved last month. Therefore, I have a new projection of another 5% increase in sales by year end.

Appendix C

Real Estate Investing for Women

Why Women Should Consider Real Estate Investing As a Career

In the real estate industry, most of the agents are women. But in the course of my career, I have met very few women who are active and successful as real estate investors. I think that's a waste of good womanpower. Here are several reasons why I think women can be outstanding real estate investors.

- The ability to listen. People love to talk and, sexism notwithstanding, women are better listeners. We devote our full attention to an individual while getting their story. We make great negotiators with our listening skills.

- Attention to detail. Women research endlessly if they are passionate about what they're trying to accomplish. Items like looking up comparables, searching the Internet for properties, and doing the final touches in staging a property for sale, are often better accomplished by a woman.

- Women are generally seen as less threatening in power situations. This can give us the advantage in having others open up to us.

- Most businesses are owned and operated by men. Women are in the support role. It's refreshing to others to view women as successful. This happens to me a lot. When I speak to real estate investor groups, the women are especially appreciative that it's a woman who's made it!

- As noted, the majority of real estate agents are women. They are friendly, persistent, and follow up with their prospects. If you can be an agent, you can be a real estate investor. If you are not an agent but are friendly, persistent, and do follow up, you can become a great real estate investor.

So why have so few women made real estate investing a hobby or, better yet, a business?

I think it's because women too often lack confidence in their abilities. When it comes to real estate investing, they may be afraid they don't have enough information to put together the deal, or afraid of dealing with banks, contractors, and others who might well practice the tactic of intimidation. They may be afraid of taking a financial risk, and instead choose to depend on others for financial security.

So, I say to potential women real estate investors: Yes, you need to learn the basics. You took that first step when you purchased this program. Now it's up to you. Here are a few points to remember as you build that business, and on a budget, no less!

- Stay in touch with fellow investors. Continue to expand your knowledge base by joining a real estate investor association or by going online, reading articles, and learning more about what you want to specialize in with your newfound career.

- Subscribe to Web sites like Creative Real Estate Online. They cover just about every type of real estate investment imaginable, and they even have a cash flow forum for seller-financed paper.

- Get out there and do something! The best illustration I have for this is my friend Barbara.

Barbara has been investing in the California real estate market since the early 1980s. We met in 1988 at a convention. Since then she has expanded her horizons to land developer, commercial real estate notes, and financing Veteran's Administration hospitals around the country. How did she do this? It wasn't with knowledge. She just jumped right in with both feet and went for it. Did she make mistakes? Sure she did. Once she made such a big mistake, I thought it would put her out of business. But that didn't stop her.

Today, Barbara is not only financially secure for the rest of her life, but she helps take care of others' financial woes. I call her UNICEF. She is a brilliant investor, not by IQ, which she also has, but by her belief that she can make the deal.

So can you. Get out there and start finding properties now! E-mail me and let me know how you are doing. And as Zig Ziglar says, "I'll see you at the top!"

Appendix D

Sample Documents

The following sample documents are found in this appendix:

1. PROPERTY INSPECTION SHEET

INSPECTION REPORT
[ ] MOVE IN   [ ] MOVE OUT

Tenant Name: _____

Address: _____

Apartment Complex: _____ Apartment No.: _____

Move-In Date: _____ Move-Out Date: _____ Date Notice Given: _____

LIVING-DINING ROOMS: 1-Good 2-Average 3-Below Average 4-Needs Attention

Floor or Carpet _____	Disposal_____
Walls and Baseboards _____	Dishwasher _____
Ceiling _____	Fan _____
Glass _____	Sink _____
Screens _____	Faucet _____
Drapes and Rods _____	Cupboards_____
Switches and Light Fixtures _____	Doors and Locks _____
Doors and Locks _____	Other _____
Closets_____	
Other _____	FIRST BATHROOM:
	Floor or Carpet _____
KITCHEN:	Walls and Baseboards _____
Floor or Carpet _____	Switches and Light Fixtures _____
Walls and Baseboards _____	Ceiling _____
Switches and Light Fixtures _____	Glass _____
Ceiling _____	Screens _____
Glass _____	Tub and/or Tile _____
Screens _____	Shower_____
Drapes and Rods _____	Faucets_____
Stove _____	Sink _____
Refrigerator _____	Toilet _____

Towel Racks _____

Cabinets_____

Curtain Rods _____

Doors and Locks _____

Other _____

SECOND BATHROOM:

Floor or Carpet _____

Walls and Baseboards _____

Switches and Light Fixtures _____

Ceiling _____

Glass _____

Screens _____

Tub and/or Tile _____

Shower_____

Faucets_____

Sink _____

Toilet _____

Towel Racks _____

Cabinets_____

Curtain Rod _____

Doors and Locks _____

FIRST BEDROOM:

Floor or Carpet _____

Walls and Baseboards _____

Switches and Light Fixtures _____

Ceiling _____

Glass _____

Screens _____

Drapes and Rods _____

Closets _____

Rods and Hooks_____

Doors and Locks _____

Other _____

SECOND BEDROOM:

Floor or Carpet _____

Walls and Baseboards _____

Switches and Light Fixtures _____

Ceiling _____

Glass _____

Drapes and Rods _____

Doors and Locks _____

Closets _____

Rods and Hooks_____

Doors and Locks _____

Other _____

THIRD BEDROOM:

Floor or Carpet _____

Walls and Baseboards _____

Switches and Light Fixtures _____

Ceiling _____

Glass _____

Screens _____

Drapes and Rods _____

Closets _____

Rods and Hooks_____

Doors and Locks _____

Other _____

LINEN CLOSET:

Doors and Locks _____

Shelves_____

Drawers_____

Rods and Hooks_____

Walls and Baseboards _____

Ceiling _____

Switches and Light Fixtures _____

OUTSIDE:

Garage or Parking Stall_____

Mailbox _____

Screen door_____

Storage _____

Yard _____

Light Fixture_____

Other _____

OTHER:

_____

_____

_____

_____

_____

_____

2. ASSIGNMENT OF RENTS

When recorded, return to:
Your name
Address
City, State zipcode

Prepared by Your Name   Space above for recorder's use

Assignment

THE UNDERSIGNED,

Your Name

being the holder in due course of the Promissory Note to which this is attached, for the sum of $10.00 and other valuable considerations, HEREBY assigns, transfers, and conveys all right, title, and interest, being the entire beneficial interest, as obligee, payee, and beneficiary under this Promissory Note, [ ] with [x] without recourse, including the security instrument originally recorded:

County: <u>County</u>
State: <u>State</u>
Payor: <u>Payor name</u>
Book/Pg: <u>Recording information</u>

securing same to <u>Your investor</u>.

WITNESS my hand and seal, April 15, 2006.

_____ (Seal)

Your name

_____ (Seal)

Your other name

_____ (Seal)

(Witness)

_____ (Seal)

(Witness)

Personal Notary:

State of _____ _____, County of _____ _____

I, _____, a Notary Public for the County and State aforesaid, do hereby certify that _____ personally appeared before me this day and duly acknowledged the execution of the foregoing instrument.

      Witness my hand and official seal, this the _____ day of _____, 20_____,

_____ . My commission expires _____, 20_____.

(Notary Public)

For official use only: State of _____, County of _____.

Each of the foregoing certificates, namely of _____, a Notary or Notaries Public of the State and County designated, is certified to be correct, this _____ day of _____, 20_____ .

_____, Register of Deeds, by:

_____

Filed for registration on the _____ day of _____, 20_____ at _____ .m.

Corporate Notary:

State of _____, County of _____.

      I, _____, a Notary Public for the County and State aforesaid, do hereby certify that _____ personally appeared before me this day and duly acknowledged that __ he is the Secretary of _____, a _____ Corporation, and that by authority duly given and as the act of the corporation, the foregoing instrument was signed in its name by its President, sealed with its corporate seal, and attested by its Secretary.

      Witness my hand and official seal, this the _____ day of _____, 20_____.

_____

(Notary Public)

My commission expires _____, 20_____.

                ****

For official use only

State of _____, County of _____.

     Each of the foregoing certificates, namely of _____

_____, a Notary or Notaries Public of the State and County designated, is certified to be correct.

     This _____ day of _____, 20_____.

_____

Register of Deeds, _____ County, by:

_____

Filed for registration on the _____ day of _____, 20_____ at _____ .m.

_____

Register of Deeds, _____ County, by:

_____

> ## 3. CLASSIFIED AD LETTER

Your Company Name
123 Main Street
Anywhere, USA 00000
(123) 456-7890

———————

«Title» «First name» «Last name»
«Company»
«Street»
«City», «State» «Zip code»

Dear «Title» «Last name»,

Here is copy for a classified ad to start as soon as possible:

If you have sold your home and taken back a
mortgage or trust deed, I will buy that mortgage
or trust deed for CASH! Call Lisa at 123-456-7890.

I would like this classified ad to run in your Money to Lend section for 8 weeks.
Enclosed is my check for $56.

If the ad does not fit in that space, let me know. Please send me a copy when it is
published, since the paper is not circulated here. Thank you.

Sincerely,

Your Name

4. CREDIT APPLICATION

Property: _____   Date: _____

Name of applicant: _____   SSN and Driver's License: _____

Cosigner: _____   SSN and Driver's License: _____

Present address: _____   Phone: _____

Amount of rent: _____Or mortgage: _____   How long: _____

Manager's name if renting: _____   Manager's phone: _____

Previous residence:

Amount of rent: _____Or mortgage: _____   How long: _____

Manager's name if rented:_____   Manager's phone: _____

Employment information:

Employer: _____   Employer phone: _____

Address:_____   Monthly salary: _____

_____   How long: _____

Cosigner employment information:

Employer: _____   Employer phone: _____

Address:_____   Monthly salary: _____

_____   How long: _____

Financial information:

Bank and branch: _____   Phone: _____

Saving account: _____   Checking account: _____

Other accounts:_____   Other assets: _____

Major credit cards: _____   Number:_____

Monthly obligations:

Car:_____   Balance and payment: _____

Child support and alimony:_____   Balance and payment: _____

Other:_____   Balance and payment: _____

Other:_____   Balance and payment: _____

Automobiles:

Make, model, year: _____   License: _____

Make, model, year: _____   License: _____

Personal references:

Name: _____   Phone: _____

Address: _____   _____

Name: _____   Phone: _____

Address: _____   _____

Please answer the following:

Are there any outstanding judgments against any applicant?   [ ] Yes   [ ] No

Has either applicant willfully and intentionally refused to pay
the rent or mortgage when due?   [ ] Yes   [ ] No

Does either applicant know of anything which may interrupt
your income or ability to pay?   [ ] Yes   [ ] No

Has either applicant ever filed a petition for bankruptcy?   [ ] Yes   [ ] No

I HEREBY AUTHORIZE YOU TO OBTAIN A CREDIT BUREAU REPORT AND I AGREE TO PAY THE REQUESTED FEE FOR THIS SERVICE. This credit report may be shared confidentially with other parties who may extend credit to me. I certify that the asnwers I have given in this application are true and correct to the best of my knowledge. Any false answers or statements made by me while applying for credit can be considered fraud.

_____   _____

Applicant's signature   Co-applicant's signature

5. CREDIT REPORT AUTHORIZATIONS

Credit Report Authorization: Simple Form

Name of Organization
Address

I hereby grant permission for the above-named organization or their assigns to obtain my credit report for their own private and confidential use.

The following information is current:

Full name: _____

Address: _____

City, State, Zip: _____ ____ _____

Telephone: (_____)_____

Soc. Sec. Num.: _____

Signature: _____

Credit Report Authorization for Someone Out of State

Name of Organization
Address

I hereby grant permission for the above-named organization or their assigns to obtain my credit report for their own private and confidential use.

The following information is current:

Full name: _____

Address: _____

City, State, Zip: _____

Telephone: (_____)_____

Soc. Sec. Num.:   _____

Signature: _____

[x] Attach a copy of your state driver's license.

[x] Have this form notarized.

BEFORE ME personally appeared _____, whose signature appears above, and is known to me to be a credible witness over the age of eighteen years.

EXECUTED this the _____day of _____, 20__.

_____

NOTARY PUBLIC IN AND FOR THE

STATE OF _____

6. DEED OF TRUST

Deed of Trust When Buying

When recorded, return to:
«First name» «Last name»
«Street»
«City», «State» «Zip code»

Prepared by Your Name   Space above for recorder's use

THIS DEED OF TRUST, dated «NoteDate», is between

<u>Your Company Name</u>
<u>Your Address</u>
<u>City, St Zip</u>

also called Borrower, and

«Trustee»

also called Trustee, for the benefit of

«First name» «Last name»
«Cosigner»
«Street»
«City», «State» «Zip code»

also called Lender.

Borrower and Lender covenant and agree as follows:

1. Property in Trust. Borrower, in consideration of the indebtedness herein recited and the trust herein created, hereby grants and coveys to Trustee in trust, with the power of sale, the following described property, «Property», situated in the county of «County».

2. Note. This Deed of Trust is given to secure to Lender:

A. the repayment of the indebtedness evidenced by Borrower's note of even date in the principal sum of $«FaceAmt» with interest on the unpaid principal balance from «NoteDate» until paid at the rate of «Rate» percent per annum with principal and interest payable at the Lender's address above or such other place as the Lender may designate, in monthly payments of $«Payment», due on the same day of each month beginning «PmtDate» and continuing until the entire indebtedness evidenced by said Note is fully paid; however, if not sooner paid, the entire principal amount outstanding, and accrued interest thereon, shall be due and payable on «Maturity»; further, Borrower agrees to pay Lender a late charge of $«LateFee» if any payment is not received by the Lender within «GraceDays» days after payment is due; and Borrower has the right to prepay the principal amount outstanding under said Note in whole or in part at any time without penalty, except as noted: None noted.

B. the payment of all other sums, with interest thereon at the note rate of «Rate» % per annum, disbursed by Lender in accordance with this Deed of Trust to protect the security of this Deed of Trust; and

C. the performance of the covenants and agreements of Borrower herein contained.

3. Title. Borrower covenants that Borrower owns and has the right to grant and convey the Property and warrants title to the same subject to general real estate taxes for the current year, easements of record or in existence, and recorded declarations, restrictions, reservations, and covenants, if any, as of this date, except as noted: None noted.

4. Payment of Principal and Interest. Borrower shall promptly pay when due the principal of and interest on the indebtedness evidenced by the Note and late charges as provided in the Note and shall perform all of Borrower's other covenants contained in the Note.

5. Application of Payments. All payments received by Lender under the terms hereof shall be applied by Lender first in payment of amounts due pursuant to paragraph 23 (Escrow Funds for Taxes and Insurance), then to amounts disbursed by Lender pursuant to paragraph 9 (Protection of Lender's Security), and the balance in accordance with the terms and conditions of the Note.

6. Prior Mortgages and Deeds of Trust, Charges, Liens. Borrower shall perform all of Borrower's obligations under any prior deed of trust and any other prior liens. Borrower shall pay all taxes, assessments, and other charges, fines and impositions attributable to the Property which may have or attain a priority over this Deed of Trust, and leasehold payments or ground rents, if any, in the manner set out in paragraph 23 (Escrow Funds for Taxes and Insurance) or, if not required to be paid in such manner, by Borrower making payment when due, directly to

Initials: _____ _____

the payee thereof. Despite the foregoing, Borrower shall not be required to make payments otherwise required by this paragraph if Borrower, after notice to Lender, shall in good faith contest such obligation by, or defend enforcement of such obligation in, legal proceedings which operate to prevent the enforcement of the obligation or forfeiture of the Property or any part thereof., only upon Borrower making all such contested payments and other payments as ordered by the court to the registry of the court in which such proceedings are filed.

7. Property Insurance. Borrower shall keep the improvements now existing or hereafter erected on the Properry insured against loss by fire, hazards included within the term "extended coverage," and any other hazards, including floods or flooding, for which Lender requires insurance. This insurance shall be maintained for the periods that Lender requires and in an amount equal to or exceeding Lender's security interest in the property, including any liens prior to Lender's lien. The insurance carrier providing the insurance shall be chosen by Borrower subject to Lender's approval which shall not be unreasonably withheld. If Borrower fails to maintain coverage described above, Lender may, at Lender's option, obtain coverage to protect Lender's rights in the Property in accordance with paragraph 7.

All insurance policies and renewals shall be acceptable to Lender and shall include a standard mortgage clause. Lender shall have the right to hold the policies and renewals. If Lender requires, Borrower shall promptly give to Lender all receipts of paid premiums and renewal notices. In the event of loss, Borrower shall give prompt notice to the insurance carrier and Lender. Lender may make proof of loss if not made promptly by Borrower.

Unless Lender and Borrower otherwise agree in writing, insurance proceeds shall be applied to restoration or repair of the Property damaged, if the restoration or repair is economically feasible and Lender's security is not lessened. If the restoration or repair is not economically feasible or Lender's security would be lessened, the insurance proceeds shall be applied to the sums secured by this Security Instrument, whether or not then due, with any excess paid to Borrower. If Borrower abandons the Property, or does not answer within 30 days a notice from Lender that the insurance carrier has offered to settle a claim, then Lender may collect the insurance proceeds. Lender may use the proceeds to repair or restore the Property or to pay sums secured by this Security Instrument, whether or not then due. The 30-day period will begin when the notice is given.

Unless Lender and Borrower otherwise agree in writing, any application of proceeds to principal shall not extend or postpone the due date of the monthly payments referred to in paragraphs 1 and 2 or change the amount of the payments. If under paragraph 21 the Property is acquired by Lender, Borrower's right to any insurance policies and proceeds resulting from damage to the Property prior to the acquisition shall pass to Lender to the extent of the sums secured by this Security Instrument immediately prior to the acquisition.

Initials: _____ _____

8. Preservation and Maintenance of Property. Borrower shall keep the Property in good repair and shall not commit waste or permit impairment or deterioration of the Property. Borrower shall perform all of Borrower's obligations under any declarations, covenants, by-laws, rules, or other documents governing the use, ownership, or occupancy of the Property.

9. Protection of Lender's Security. Except when Borrower has exercised Borrower's rights under paragraph 6 above, if the Borrower fails to perform the covenants and agreements contained in this Deed of Trust, or if a default occurs in a prior lien, or if any action or proceeding is commenced which materially affects Lender's interest in the Property, then Lender, at Lender's option, with notice to Borrower if required by law, may make such appearances, disburse such sums, and take such actions as is necessary to protect Lender's interest, including, but not limited to, disbursement of reasonable attorney's fees and entry upon the Property to make repairs. Borrower hereby assigns to Lender any right Borrower may have by reason of any prior encumbrance on the Property or by law or otherwise to cure any default under said prior encumbrance.

Any amounts disbursed by Lender pursuant to this paragraph 9, with interest thereon, shall become additional indebtedness of Borrower secured by this Deed of Trust. Such amounts shall be payable upon notice from Lender to Borrower requesting payment thereof, and Lender may bring suit to collect any amounts so disbursed plus interest specified in paragraph 2B (Note; Other Obligations Secured). Nothing contained in this paragraph 9 shall require Lender to incur any expense or take any action hereunder.

10. Inspection. Lender or its agent may make reasonable entries upon and inspections of the Property. Lender shall give Borrower notice at the time of or prior to an inspection specifying reasonable cause for the inspection.

11. Condemnation. The proceeds of any award or claim for damages, direct or consequential, in connection with any condemnation or other taking of any part of the Property, or for conveyance in lieu of condemnation, are hereby assigned and shall be paid to Lender.

In the event of a total taking of the Property, the proceeds shall be applied to the sums secured by this Security Instrument, whether or not then due, with any excess paid to Borrower. In the event of a partial taking of the Property in which the fair market value of the Property immediately before the taking is equal to or greater than the amount of the sums secured by this Security Instrument immediately before the taking, unless Borrower and Lender otherwise agree in writing, the sums secured by this Security Instrument shall be reduced by the amount of the proceeds multiplied by the following fraction: (a) the total amount of the sums secured immediately before the taking, divided by (b) the fair market value of the Property immediately before the taking. Any balance shall be paid to Borrower. In the event of a partial taking of the Property in

Initials: _____   _____

which the fair market value of the Property immediately before the taking is less than the amount of the sums secured immediately before the taking, unless Borrower and Lender otherwise agree in writing or unless applicable law otherwise provides, the proceeds shall be applied to the sums secured by this Security Instrument whether or not the sums are then due.

If the Property is abandoned by Borrower, or if, after notice by Lender to Borrower that the condemnor offers to make an award or settle a claim for damages, Borrower fails to respond to Lender within 30 days after the date the notice is given, Lender is authorized to collect and apply the proceeds, at its option, either to restoration or repair of the Property or to the sums secured by this Security Instrument, whether or not then due.

Unless Lender and Borrower otherwise agree in writing, any application of proceeds to principal shall not extend or postpone the due date of the monthly payments referred to in paragraph 2 or change the amount of such payments.

12. Borrower Not Released. Extension of the time for payment or modification of amortization of the sums secured by this Deed of Trust granted by Lender to any successor in interest of Borrower shall not operate to release, in any manner, the liability of the original Borrower, nor Borrower's successors in interest, from the original terms of this Deed of Trust. Lender shall not be required to commence proceedings against such successor or refuse to extend time for payment or otherwise modify amortization of the sums secured by this Deed of Trust by reason of any demand made by the original Borrower nor Borrower's successors in interest.

13. Forbearance by Lender Not a Waiver. Any forbearance by Lender in exercising any right or remedy hereunder, or otherwise afforded by law, shall not be a waiver or preclude the exercise of any such right or remedy.

14. Remedies Cumulative. Each remedy provided in the Note and this Deed of Trust is distinct from and cumulative to all other rights or remedies under the Note and this Deed of Trust or afforded by law or equity, and may be exercised concurrently, independently, or successively.

15. Successors and Assigns Bound; Joint and Several Liability; Captions. The covenants and agreements herein contained shall bind, and the rights hereunder shall inure to, the respective successors and assigns of Lender and Borrower, subject to the provisions of paragraph 24 (Transfer of the Property; Assumption). All covenants and agreements of Borrower shall be joint and several. The captions and headings of the paragraphs in this Deed of Trust are for convenience only and are not to be used to interpret or define the provisions hereof.

16. Notice. Except for any notice required by law to be given in another manner, (a) any notice to Borrower provided for in this Deed of Trust shall be in writing and shall be given and be effec-

Initials: _____ _____

tive upon delivery to Borrower or mailing such notice by first-class U.S. mail, addressed to Borrower at Borrower's address stated herein or at such other address as Borrower may designate by notice to Lender as provided herein, and (b) any notice to Lender shall be in writing and shall be given and be effective upon delivery to Lender or mailing such notice by first-class U.S. mail, to Lender's address stated herein or to such other address as Lender may designate by notice to Borrower as provided herein. Any notice provided for in this Deed of Trust shall be deemed to have been given to Borrower or Lender when given in any manner designated herein.

17. Governing Law; Severability. The Note and this Deed of Trust shall be governed by the law of the state in which the property is located. In the event that any provision or clause of this Deed of Trust or the Note conflicts with the law, such conflict shall not affect other provisions of this Deed of Trust or the Note which can be given effect without the conflicting provision, and to this end the provisions of the Deed of Trust and Note are declared to be severable.

18. Acceleration; Foreclosure; Other Remedies. Except as provided in paragraph 24 (Transfer of the Property; Assumption), upon Borrower's breach of any covenant or agreement of Borrower in this Deed of Trust, or upon any default in a prior lien upon the Property (unless Borrower has exercised Borrower's rights under paragraph 6 above), at Lender's option, all of the sums secured by this Deed of Trust shall be immediately due and payable (Acceleration). To exercise this option, Lender may invoke the power of sale and any other remedies permitted by law. Lender shall be entitled to collect all reasonable costs and expenses incurred in pursuing the remedies provided in this Deed of Trust, including, but not limited to, reasonable attorney's fees.

If Lender invokes the power of sale, Lender shall give written notice to Trustee of such election. Trustee shall give such notice to Borrower of Borrower's rights as is provided by law. Trustee shall record a copy of such notice as required by law. Trustee shall advertise the time and place of the sale of the Property for not less than four weeks in a newspaper of general circulation in each county in which the Property is situated, and shall mail copies of such notice of sale to Borrower and other persons as prescribed by law. After the lapse of such time as may be required by law, Trustee, without demand on Borrower, shall sell the Property at public auction to the highest bidder for cash at the time and place (which may be on the Property or any part thereof as permitted by law) in one or more parcels as Trustee may think best and in such order as Trustee may determine. Lender or Lender's designee may purchase the Property at any sale. It shall not be obligatory upon the purchaser at any such sale to see to the application of the purchase money.

Trustee shall apply the proceeds of the sale in the following order: (a) to all reasonable costs and expenses of the sale, including, but not limited to, reasonable Trustee's and attorney's fees

Initials: _____ _____

and costs of title evidence; (b) to all sums secured by this Deed of Trust; and (c) the excess, if any, to the person or persons legally entitled thereto.

19. Borrower's Right to Cure Default. Whenever foreclosure is commenced for nonpayment of any sums due hereunder, the owners of the Property or parties liable hereon shall be entitled to cure said defaults by paying all delinquent principal and interest payments due as of the date of cure, costs, expenses, late charges, attorney's fees, and other fees all in the manner provided by law. Upon such payment, this Deed of Trust and the obligations secured hereby shall remain in full force and effect as though no Acceleration had occurred, and the foreclosure proceedings shall be discontinued.

20. Assignment of Rents; Appointment of Receiver; Lender in Possession. As additional security hereunder, Borrower hereby assigns to Lender the rents of the Property; however, Borrower shall, prior to Acceleration under paragraph 18 (Acceleration; Foreclosure; Other Remedies) or abandonment of the Property, have the right to collect and retain such rents as they become due and payable. Lender or the holder of the Trustee's certificate of purchase shall be entitled to a receiver for the Property after Acceleration under paragraph 18 (Acceleration; Foreclosure; Other Remedies) and shall also be so entitled during the time covered by foreclosure proceedings and the period of redemption, if any, and shall be entitled thereto as a matter of right without regard to the solvency or insolvency of Borrower or of the then owner of the Property, and without regard to the value thereof. Such receiver may be appointed by any Court of competent jurisdiction upon *ex parte* application and without notice, notice being hereby expressly waived.

Upon Acceleration under paragraph 18 (Acceleration; Foreclosure; Other Remedies) or abandonment of the Property, Lender, in person, by agent, or by judicially appointed receiver, shall be entitled to enter upon, take possession of, and manage the Property and to collect the rents of the Property including those past due. All rents collected by Lender or the receiver shall be applied first to payment of the costs of preservation and management of the Property; second to payments due upon prior liens, and then to the sums secured by this Deed of Trust. Lender and the receiver shall be liable to account only for those rents actually received.

21. Release. Upon payment of all sums secured by this Deed of Trust, Lender shall cause Trustee to release this Deed of Trust and shall produce for Trustee the Note. Lender shall pay all costs of recordation and shall pay the statutory Trustee's fees. If Lender shall not produce the Note as aforesaid, then Lender, upon notice in accordance with paragraph 16 (Notice) from Borrower to Lender, shall obtain and file, at Lender's expense, any lost instrument bond required by Trustee or pay the cost thereof to effect the release of this Deed of Trust.

Initials: _____   _____

22. Waiver of Exemptions. Borrower hereby waives all right of homestead and any other exemption in the Property under state or federal law presently existing or hereafter enacted.

23. Escrow Funds for Taxes and Insurance. Borrower agrees to pay property taxes in a timely manner and maintain a hazard insurance policy in an amount equal to or greater than the principal balance of the note. Upon request by the Lender, Borrower agrees to provide a receipt for the property taxes or hazard insurance showing that each amount has been timely paid.

24. Transfer of the Property: Assumption, Release of Liability, Property Sole Security. The following events shall be referred to herein as a "Transfer":
(i) a transfer or conveyance of title (or any portion thereof, legal or equitable) of the Property (or any part thereof or interest therein),
(ii) the execution of a contract or agreement creating a right to title (or any portion thereof, legal or equitable) in the Property (or any part thereof or interest therein),
(iii) an agreement granting a possessory right in the Property (or any portion thereof) in excess of three (3) years,
(iv) a sale or transfer of, or the execution of a contract or agreement creating a right to acquire or receive more than fifty percent (50%) of, the controlling interest or more than fifty percent (50%) of the beneficial interest in the Borrower, or
(v) the reorganization, liquidation, or dissolution of the Borrower.

Not to be included as a Transfer are:
(i) the creation of a lien or encumbrance subordinate to this Deed of Trust,
(ii) the creation of a purchase money security interest for household appliances, or
(iii) a transfer by devise, descent, or by operation of the law upon the death of a joint tenant.

Lender specifically agrees to allow the assumption of this deed of trust by a creditworthy entity, such creditworthiness to be solely determined at Lender's discretion by comparing the assuming entity's credit bureau report to the existing Borrower's credit bureau report. Upon such approval, Lender agrees to provide Borrower with a written release from liability.

25. Sole Security. Lender acknowledges that the property secured by this deed of trust shall be the sole security for the repayment of its associated note.

26. Loan Charges. If the loan secured by this Security Instrument is subject to a law which sets maximum loan charges, and that law is finally interpreted so that the interest or other loan charges collected or to be collected in connection with the loan exceed the permitted limits, then: (a) any such loan charge shall be reduced by the amount necessary to reduce the charge to the permitted limit, and (b) any sums already collected from Borrower which exceeded permitted limits will be refunded to Borrower. Lender may choose to make this refund by reduc-

Initials: _____   _____

ing the principal owed under the Note or by making a direct payment to Borrower. If a refund reduces principal, the reduction will be treated as a partial prepayment without any prepayment charge under the Note.

27. Legal Implications. This agreement is a legal instrument. You should consult your legal or tax advisor before signing this agreement.

28. Borrower's Copy. Borrower acknowledges receipt of a copy of this deed of trust and its referenced note.

WITNESS my hand and seal,   April 15, 2006.

_____ Seal   _____

Buyer: Your Name   Witness

_____ Seal   _____

Buyer: Cosigner   Witness

Personal Notary:

State of _____, County of _____.

I, _____, a Notary Public for the County and State aforesaid, do hereby certify that _____ personally appeared before me this day and duly acknowledged the execution of the foregoing instrument.

   Witness my hand and official seal, this the _____ day of _____, 20_____,

_____ . My commission expires _____, 20_____.

(Notary Public)

Corporate notary

State of _____, County of _____.

   I, _____, a Notary Public for the County and State aforesaid, do hereby certify that _____ personally appeared before me this day and duly acknowledged that __he is the Secretary of _____, a _____ Corporation, and that by authority duly given and as the act of the corporation, the foregoing instrument was signed in its name by its President, sealed with its corporate seal, and attested by its Secretary.

Initials: _____ _____

Witness my hand and official seal, this the _____ day of _____, 20_____.

_____

(Notary Public)

My commission expires _____, 20_____.

****

For official use only

State of _____, County of _____.

Each of the foregoing certificates, namely of _____
_____, a Notary or Notaries Public of the State and County designated, is certified to be correct.

This _____ day of _____, 20_____.

_____

Register of Deeds, _____ County, by: _____

Filed for registration on the _____ day of _____, 20_____ at _____ .m.

_____

Register of Deeds, _____ County, by: _____

Initials: _____ _____

Deed of Trust When Selling

When recorded, return to:
Your Name
Address
City, State Zipcode

Prepared by Your Name   Space above for recorder's use

THIS DEED OF TRUST, dated «NoteDate», is between

«First name» «Last name»
«Cosigner»
«Street»
«City», «State» «Zip code»

also called Borrower, and

«Trustee»

also called Trustee, for the benefit of

Your Company Name
Your Address
City, St Zip

also called Lender.

Borrower and Lender covenant and agree as follows:

1. Property in Trust. Borrower, in consideration of the indebtedness herein recited and the trust herein created, hereby grants and coveys to Trustee in trust, with the power of sale, the following described property, «Property», situated in the county of «County».

2. Note. Other Obligation Secured. This Deed of Trust is given to secure to Lender:

A. the repayment of the indebtedness evidenced by Borrower's note of even date in the principal sum of $«FaceAmt» with interest on the unpaid principal balance from «NoteDate» until paid at the rate of «Rate» percent per annum with principal and interest payable at the Lender's address above or such other place as the Lender may designate, in monthly payments of $«Payment», due on the same day of each month beginning «PmtDate» and continuing until

Initials: _____ _____

the entire indebtedness evidenced by said Note is fully paid; however, if not sooner paid, the entire principal amount outstanding, and accrued interest thereon, shall be due and payable on «Maturity»; further, Borrower agrees to pay Lender a late charge of $«LateFee» if any payment is not received by the Lender within «GraceDays» days after payment is due; and Borrower has the right to prepay the principal amount outstanding under said Note in whole or in part at any time without penalty, except as noted: <u>None noted</u>.

B. the payment of all other sums, with interest thereon at the rate of «DefaultRate», disbursed by Lender in accordance with this Deed of Trust to protect the security of this Deed of Trust; and

C. the performance of the covenants and agreements of Borrower herein contained.

3. Title. Borrower covenants that Borrower owns and has the right to grant and convey the Property and warrants title to the same subject to general real estate taxes for the current year, easements of record or in existence, and recorded declarations, restrictions, reservations, and covenants, if any, as of this date, except as noted: <u>None noted</u>.

4. Payment of Principal and Interest. Borrower shall promptly pay when due the principal of and interest on the indebtedness evidenced by the Note and late charges as provided in the Note and shall perform all of Borrower's other covenants contained in the Note.

5. Application of Payments. All payments received by Lender under the terms hereof shall be applied by Lender first in payment of amounts due pursuant to paragraph 23 (Escrow Funds for Taxes and Insurance), then to amounts disbursed by Lender pursuant to paragraph 9 (Protection of Lender's Security), then to accrued late charges, and the balance in accordance with the terms and conditions of the Note.

6. Prior Mortgages and Deeds of Trust, Charges, Liens. Borrower shall perform all of Borrower's obligations under any prior deed of trust and any other prior liens. Borrower shall pay all taxes, assessments, and other charges, fines, and impositions attributable to the Property which may have or attain a priority over this Deed of Trust, and leasehold payments or ground rents, if any, in the manner set out in paragraph 23 (Escrow Funds for Taxes and Insurance) or, if not required to be paid in such manner, by Borrower making payment when due, directly to the payee thereof. Despite the foregoing, Borrower shall not be required to make payments otherwise required by this paragraph if Borrower, after notice to Lender, shall in good faith contest such obligation by, or defend enforcement of such obligation in, legal proceedings which operate to prevent the enforcement of the obligation or forfeiture of the Property or any part thereof, only upon Borrower making all such contested payments and other payments as ordered by the court to the registry of the court in which such proceedings are filed.

Initials: _____ _____

7. Property Insurance. Borrower shall keep the improvements now existing or hereafter erected on the Properry insured against loss by fire, hazards included within the term "extended coverage," and any other hazards, including floods or flooding, for which Lender requires insurance. This insurance shall be maintained for the periods that Lender requires and in an amount equal to or exceeding Lender's security interest in the property, including any liens prior to Lender's lien. The insurance carrier providing the insurance shall be chosen by Borrower subject to Lender's approval which shall not be unreasonably withheld. If Borrower fails to maintain coverage described above, Lender may, at Lender's option, obtain coverage to protect Lender's rights in the Property in accordance with paragraph 7.

All insurance policies and renewals shall be acceptable to Lender and shall include a standard mortgage clause. Lender shall have the right to hold the policies and renewals. If Lender requires, Borrower shall promptly give to Lender all receipts of paid premiums and renewal notices. In the event of loss, Borrower shall give prompt notice to the insurance carrier and Lender. Lender may make proof of loss if not made promptly by Borrower.

Unless Lender and Borrower otherwise agree in writing, insurance proceeds shall be applied to restoration or repair of the Property damaged, if the restoration or repair is economically feasible and Lender's security is not lessened. If the restoration or repair is not economically feasible or Lender's security would be lessened, the insurance proceeds shall be applied to the sums secured by this Security Instrument, whether or not then due, with any excess paid to Borrower. If Borrower abandons the Property, or does not answer within 30 days a notice from Lender that the insurance carrier has offered to settle a claim, then Lender may collect the insurance proceeds. Lender may use the proceeds to repair or restore the Property or to pay sums secured by this Security Instrument, whether or not then due. The 30-day period will begin when the notice is given.

Unless Lender and Borrower otherwise agree in writing, any application of proceeds to principal shall not extend or postpone the due date of the monthly payments referred to in paragraphs 1 and 2 or change the amount of the payments. If under paragraph 21 the Property is acquired by Lender, Borrower's right to any insurance policies and proceeds resulting from damage to the Property prior to the acquisition shall pass to Lender to the extent of the sums secured by this Security Instrument immediately prior to the acquisition.

8. Preservation and Maintenance of Property. Borrower shall keep the Property in good repair and shall not commit waste or permit impairment or deterioration of the Property. Borrower shall perform all of Borrower's obligations under any declarations, covenants, by-laws, rules, or other documents governing the use, ownership, or occupancy of the Property.

Initials: _____ _____

9. Protection of Lender's Security. Except when Borrower has exercised Borrower's rights under paragraph 6 above, if the Borrower fails to perform the covenants and agreements contained in this Deed of Trust, or if a default occurs in a prior lien, or if any action or proceeding is commenced which materially affects Lender's interest in the Property, then Lender, at Lender's option, with notice to Borrower if required by law, may make such appearances, disburse such sums, and take such actions as is necessary to protect Lender's interest, including, but not limited to, disbursement of reasonable attorney's fees and entry upon the Property to make repairs. Borrower hereby assigns to Lender any right Borrower may have by reason of any prior encumbrance on the Property or by law or otherwise to cure any default under said prior encumbrance.

Any amounts disbursed by Lender pursuant to this paragraph 9, with interest thereon, shall become additional indebtedness of Borrower secured by this Deed of Trust. Such amounts shall be payable upon notice from Lender to Borrower requesting payment thereof, and Lender may bring suit to collect any amounts so disbursed plus interest specified in paragraph 2B (Note; Other Obligations Secured). Nothing contained in this paragraph 9 shall require Lender to incur any expense or take any action hereunder.

10. Inspection. Lender or its agent may make reasonable entries upon and inspections of the Property. Lender shall give Borrower notice at the time of or prior to an inspection specifying reasonable cause for the inspection.

11. Condemnation. The proceeds of any award or claim for damages, direct or consequential, in connection with any condemnation or other taking of any part of the Property, or for conveyance in lieu of condemnation, are hereby assigned and shall be paid to Lender.

In the event of a total taking of the Property, the proceeds shall be applied to the sums secured by this Security Instrument, whether or not then due, with any excess paid to Borrower. In the event of a partial taking of the Property in which the fair market value of the Property immediately before the taking is equal to or greater than the amount of the sums secured by this Security Instrument immediately before the taking, unless Borrower and Lender otherwise agree in writing, the sums secured by this Security Instrument shall be reduced by the amount of the proceeds multiplied by the following fraction: (a) the total amount of the sums secured immediately before the taking, divided by (b) the fair market value of the Property immediately before the taking. Any balance shall be paid to Borrower. In the event of a partial taking of the Property in which the fair market value of the Property immediately before the taking is less than the amount of the sums secured immediately before the taking, unless Borrower and Lender otherwise agree in writing or unless applicable law otherwise provides, the proceeds shall be applied to the sums secured by this Security Instrument whether or not the sums are then due.

Initials: _____ _____

If the Property is abandoned by Borrower, or if, after notice by Lender to Borrower that the condemnor offers to make an award or settle a claim for damages, Borrower fails to respond to Lender within 30 days after the date the notice is given, Lender is authorized to collect and apply the proceeds, at its option, either to restoration or repair of the Property or to the sums secured by this Security Instrument, whether or not then due.

Unless Lender and Borrower otherwise agree in writing, any application of proceeds to principal shall not extend or postpone the due date of the monthly payments referred to in paragraph 2 or change the amount of such payments.

12. Borrower Not Released. Extension of the time for payment or modification of amortization of the sums secured by this Deed of Trust granted by Lender to any successor in interest of Borrower shall not operate to release, in any manner, the liability of the original Borrower, nor Borrower's successors in interest, from the original terms of this Deed of Trust. Lender shall not be required to commence proceedings against such successor or refuse to extend time for payment or otherwise modify amortization of the sums secured by this Deed of Trust by reason of any demand made by the original Borrower nor Borrower's successors in interest.

13. Forbearance by Lender Not a Waiver. Any forbearance by Lender in exercising any right or remedy hereunder, or otherwise afforded by law, shall not be a waiver or preclude the exercise of any such right or remedy.

14. Remedies Cumulative. Each remedy provided in the Note and this Deed of Trust is distinct from and cumulative to all other rights or remedies under the Note and this Deed of Trust or afforded by law or equity, and may be exercised concurrently, independently, or successively.

15. Successors and Assigns Bound; Joint and Several Liability; Captions. The covenants and agreements herein contained shall bind, and the rights hereunder shall inure to, the respective successors and assigns of Lender and Borrower, subject to the provisions of paragraph 24 (Transfer of the Property; Assumption). All covenants and agreements of Borrower shall be joint and several. The captions and headings of the paragraphs in this Deed of Trust are for convenience only and are not to be used to interpret or define the provisions hereof.

16. Notice. Except for any notice required by law to be given in another manner, (a) any notice to Borrower provided for in this Deed of Trust shall be in writing and shall be given and be effective upon delivery to Borrower or mailing such notice by first-class U.S. mail, addressed to Borrower at Borrower's address stated herein or at such other address as Borrower may designate by notice to Lender as provided herein, and (b) any notice to Lender shall be in writing and shall be given and be effective upon delivery to Lender or mailing such notice by first-class U.S. mail, to Lender's address stated herein or to such other address as Lender may

Initials: _____ _____

designate by notice to Borrower as provided herein. Any notice provided for in this Deed of Trust shall be deemed to have been given to Borrower or Lender when given in any manner designated herein.

17. Governing Law; Severability. The Note and this Deed of Trust shall be governed by the law of the state in which the property is located. In the event that any provision or clause of this Deed of Trust or the Note conflicts with the law, such conflict shall not affect other provisions of this Deed of Trust or the Note which can be given effect without the conflicting provision, and to this end the provisions of the Deed of Trust and Note are declared to be severable.

18. Acceleration; Foreclosure; Other Remedies. Except as provided in paragraph 24 (Transfer of the Property; Assumption), upon Borrower's breach of any covenant or agreement of Borrower in this Deed of Trust, or upon any default in a prior lien upon the Property (unless Borrower has exercised Borrower's rights under paragraph 6 above), at Lender's option, all of the sums secured by this Deed of Trust shall be immediately due and payable (Acceleration). To exercise this option, Lender may invoke the power of sale and any other remedies permitted by law. Lender shall be entitled to collect all reasonable costs and expenses incurred in pursuing the remedies provided in this Deed of Trust, including, but not limited to, reasonable attorney's fees.

If Lender invokes the power of sale, Lender shall give written notice to Trustee of such election. Trustee shall give such notice to Borrower of Borrower's rights as is provided by law. Trustee shall record a copy of such notice as required by law. Trustee shall advertise the time and place of the sale of the Property for not less than four weeks in a newspaper of general circulation in each county in which the Property is situated, and shall mail copies of such notice of sale to Borrower and other persons as prescribed by law. After the lapse of such time as may be required by law, Trustee, without demand on Borrower, shall sell the Property at public auction to the highest bidder for cash at the time and place (which may be on the Property or any part thereof as permitted by law) in one or more parcels as Trustee may think best and in such order as Trustee may determine. Lender or Lender's designee may purchase the Property at any sale. It shall not be obligatory upon the purchaser at any such sale to see to the application of the purchase money.

Trustee shall apply the proceeds of the sale in the following order: (a) to all reasonable costs and expenses of the sale, including, but not limited to, reasonable Trustee's and attorney's fees and costs of title evidence; (b) to all sums secured by this Deed of Trust; and (c) the excess, if any, to the person or persons legally entitled thereto.

19. Borrower's Right to Cure Default. Whenever foreclosure is commenced for nonpayment of any sums due hereunder, the owners of the Property or parties liable hereon shall be entitled

Initials: _____   _____

to cure said defaults by paying all delinquent principal and interest payments due as of the date of cure, costs, expenses, late charges, attorney's fees, and other fees all in the manner provided by law. Upon such payment, this Deed of Trust and the obligations secured hereby shall remain in full force and effect as though no Acceleration had occurred, and the foreclosure proceedings shall be discontinued.

20. Assignment of Rents; Appointment of Receiver; Lender in Possession. As additional security hereunder, Borrower hereby assigns to Lender the rents of the Property; however, Borrower shall, prior to Acceleration under paragraph 18 (Acceleration; Foreclosure; Other Remedies) or abandonment of the Property, have the right to collect and retain such rents as they become due and payable. Lender or the holder of the Trustee's certificate of purchase shall be entitled to a receiver for the Property after Acceleration under paragraph 18 (Acceleration; Foreclosure; Other Remedies) and shall also be so entitled during the time covered by foreclosure proceedings and the period of redemption, if any, and shall be entitled thereto as a matter of right without regard to the solvency or insolvency of Borrower or of the then owner of the Property, and without regard to the value thereof. Such receiver may be appointed by any Court of competent jurisdiction upon *ex parte* application and without notice, notice being hereby expressly waived.

Upon Acceleration under paragraph 18 (Acceleration; Foreclosure; Other Remedies) or abandonment of the Property, Lender, in person, by agent, or by judicially appointed receiver, shall be entitled to enter upon, take possession of, and manage the Property and to collect the rents of the Property including those past due. All rents collected by Lender or the receiver shall be applied first to payment of the costs of preservation and management of the Property; second to payments due upon prior liens; and then to the sums secured by this Deed of Trust. Lender and the receiver shall be liable to account only for those rents actually received.

21. Release. Upon payment of all sums secured by this Deed of Trust, Lender shall cause Trustee to release this Deed of Trust and shall produce for Trustee the Note. Borrower shall pay all costs of recordation and shall pay the statutory Trustee's fees. If Lender shall not produce the Note as aforesaid, then Lender, upon notice in accordance with paragraph 16 (Notice) from Borrower to Lender, shall obtain and file, at Lender's expense, any lost instrument bond required by Trustee or pay the cost thereof to effect the release of this Deed of Trust.

22. Waiver of Exemptions. Borrower hereby waives all right of homestead and any other exemption in the Property under state or federal law presently existing or hereafter enacted.

23. Escrow Funds for Taxes and Insurance. This paragraph 23 is not applicable if Funds as defined below are being paid pursuant to a prior encumbrance. Subject to applicable law,

Initials: _____ _____

Borrower shall pay to Lender on each day installments of principal and interest are payable under the Note, until the Note is paid in full, a sum herein referred to as "Funds" equal to $«Escrow», which is 1/12 of the yearly taxes and assessments which may attain priority over this Deed of Trust, plus 1/12 of yearly premium installments for Property Insurance, all as reasonably estimated initially and from time to time by Lender on the basis of assessments and bills and reasonable estimates thereof, taking into account any excess Funds not used or shortages.

The principal of the Funds shall be held in a separate account by the Lender in trust for the benefit of the Borrower and deposited in an institution the deposits or accounts of which are insured or guaranteed by a federal or state agency. Lender shall apply the Funds to pay said taxes, assessments, and insurance premiums. Lender may not charge for so holding and applying the Funds, analyzing said account, or verifying and compiling said assessments and bills. Lender shall not be required to pay Borrower any interest or earnings on the Funds. Lender shall give to Borrower, without charge, an annual accounting of the Funds showing credits and debits to the Funds and the purpose for which each debit to the Funds was made. The Funds are pledged as additional security for the sums secured by this Deed of Trust. If the amount of the Funds held by Lender shall not be sufficient to pay taxes, assessments, and insurance premiums as they fall due, Borrower shall pay to Lender any amount necessary to make up the deficiency within 30 days from the date notice is given in accordance with paragraph 16 (Notice) by Lender to Borrower requesting payment thereof, and Lender then may increase the amount of Funds at any time to eliminate any expected deficiency before the next expected disbursement.

Upon payment in full of all sums secured by this Deed of Trust, Lender shall simultaneously refund to Borrower any Funds held by Lender. If under paragraph 18 (Acceleration; Foreclosure; Other Remedies) the Property is sold or the Property is otherwise acquired by Lender, Lender shall apply, no later than immediately prior to the sale of the Property or its acquisition by Lender, whichever occurs first, any Funds held by Lender at the time of application as a credit against the sums secured by this Deed of Trust.

24. Transfer of the Property: Assumption. The following events shall be referred to herein as a "Transfer":
(i) a transfer or conveyance of title (or any portion thereof, legal or equitable) of the Property (or any part thereof or interest therein),
(ii) the execution of a contract or agreement creating a right to title (or any portion thereof, legal or equitable) in the Property (or any part thereof or interest therein),
(iii) an agreement granting a possessory right in the Property (or any portion thereof) in excess of three (3) years,

Initials: _____ _____

26. Legal Implications. This agreement is a legal instrument. You should consult your legal or tax advisor before signing this agreement.

27. Borrower's Copy. Borrower acknowledges receipt of a copy of this deed of trust and its referenced note.

WITNESS my hand and seal,   _____

_____ Seal   _____

Buyer: «First name» «Last name»   Witness

_____ Seal   _____

Buyer: «Cosigner»   Witness

Personal Notary:

State of _____, County of _____.

I, _____, a Notary Public for the County and State aforesaid, do hereby certify that _____ personally appeared before me this day and duly acknowledged the execution of the foregoing instrument.

Witness my hand and official seal, this the _____ day of _____, 20_____.

_____ . My commission expires _____, 20_____.

(Notary Public)

Corporate Notary

State of _____, County of _____.

I, _____, a Notary Public for the County and State aforesaid, do hereby certify that _____ personally appeared before me this day and duly acknowledged that __he is the Secretary of _____, a _____ Corporation, and that by authority duly given and as the act of the corporation, the foregoing instrument was signed in its name by its President, sealed with its corporate seal, and attested by its Secretary.

Initials: _____   _____

Witness my hand and official seal, this the _____ day of _____, 20_____.

_____

(Notary Public)

My commission expires _____, 20_____.

****

<u>For official use only</u>

State of _____, County of _____.

Each of the foregoing certificates, namely of _____
_____, a Notary or Notaries Public of the State and County designated, is certified to be correct.

This _____ day of _____, 20_____.

_____

Register of Deeds, _____ County, by: _____

Filed for registration on the _____ day of _____, 20_____ at _____ .m.

_____

Register of Deeds, _____ County, by: _____

Initials: _____ _____

7. WARRANTY DEEDS

Warranty Deed When Buying

When recorded, return to:
Your name
Address
City, St Zip

Prepared by Your Name   Space above for recorder's use

THIS DEED, dated «NoteDate», made between:

«First name» «Last name»
«Cosigner»
«Street»
«City», «State» «Zip code»

also called the Grantor, and:

Your Company Name
Your Address
City, St Zip

also called the Grantee, Witnesseth, that the Grantor, for the sum of $10.00 and other considerations, the receipt and sufficiency of which is hereby acknowledged, has granted, bargained, sold, and conveyed, and by these present. does grant, bargain, sell, convey, and confirm unto the grantee, his heirs and assigns forever, all the real property, together with improvements, if any, situate, lying, and being in the County of «County» and State of «PropState», described as follows:

«Legal»

also known as «Property».

TOGETHER with all and singular the hereditaments and appurtenances thereto belonging, or in any way appertaining and the reversion and reversions, remainder and remainders, rents, issues, and profits thereof, and all the estate, right, title, interest, claim, and demand whatsoever of the grantor, either in law or equity, of, in, and to the above bargained premises, with the hereditaments and appurtenances.

TO HAVE AND TO HOLD the said premises above bargained and described, with the appurtenances, unto the grantee, his heirs and assigns forever. And the grantor, for himself, his heirs and personal representatives, does covenant, grant, bargain, and agree to and with the grantee, his heirs and assigns, that at the time of the ensealing and delivery of these presents, he is well seized of the premises above conveyed, has good, sure, perfect, absolute, and indefeasible estate of inheritance, in law, in fee simple, and has good right, full power, and lawful authority to grant, bargain, sell, and convey the same in manner and form as aforesaid, and that the same are free and clear from all former and other grants, bar~ains, sales, liens, taxes, assessments, encumbrances, and restrictions of whatever kind or nature soever, except general taxes for 1994 and subsequent years; except easements, restrictions, covenants, conditions, reservations, and rights of way of record, if any;

      <u>None noted.</u>

The grantor shall and will WARRANT AND FOREVER DEFEND the above-bargained premises in the quiet and peaceable possession of the grantee, his heirs assigns, against all and every person or persons lawfully claiming the whole or any part thereof. The singular number shall include the plural, the plural the singular, and the use of any gender shall be applicable to all genders.

IN WITNESS WHEREOF the grantor has executed this deed on the date set forth above.

_____ Seal   _____

Grantor: «First name» «Last name»   Witness

_____ Seal   _____

Co-Grantor: «Cosigner»   Witness

<u>Personal Notary:</u>

State of _____, County of _____.

I, _____, a Notary Public for the County and State aforesaid, do hereby certify that _____ personally appeared before me this day and duly acknowledged the execution of the foregoing instrument.

      Witness my hand and official seal, this the _____ day of _____, 19_____,

_____ . My commission expires _____, 19_____.

(Notary Public)

Corporate notary

State of _____, County of _____.

  I, _____, a Notary Public for the County and State aforesaid, do hereby certify that _____
personally appeared before me this day and duly acknowledged that __he is the Secretary of _____, a _____ Corporation, and that by authority duly given and as the act of the corporation, the foregoing instrument was signed in its name by its President, sealed with its corporate seal, and attested by its Secretary.

  Witness my hand and official seal, this the _____ day of _____, 19_____.

_____

(Notary Public)

My commission expires _____, 19_____.

       ****

For official use only

State of _____, County of _____.

  Each of the foregoing certificates, namely of _____
_____, a Notary or Notaries Public of the State and County designated, is certified to be correct.

  This _____ day of _____, 19_____.

_____

Register of Deeds, _____ County, by: _____

Filed for registration on the _____ day of _____, 19_____ at _____ .m.

_____

Register of Deeds, _____ County, by: _____

Warranty Deed When Selling

When recorded, return to:
«First name» «Last name»
«Street»
«City», «State» «Zip code»

Prepared by Your Name   Space above for recorder's use

THIS DEED, dated «NoteDate», made between:

Your Company Name
Your Address
City, St Zip

also called the Grantor, and:

«First name» «Last name»
«Cosigner»
«Street»
«City», «State» «Zip code»

also called the Grantee, Witnesseth, that the Grantor, for the sum of $10.00 and other consid-erations, the receipt and sufficiency of which is hereby acknowledged, has granted, bargained, sold, and conveyed, and by these present. does grant, bargain, sell, convey, and confirm unto the grantee, his heirs and assigns forever, all the real property, together with improvements, if any, situate, lying, and being in the County of «County» and State of «PropState», described as follows:

«Legal»

also known as «Property».

TOGETHER with all and singular the hereditaments and appurtenances thereto belonging, or in any way appertaining and the reversion and reversions, remainder and remainders, rents, issues, and profits thereof, and all the estate, right, title, interest, claim, and demand whatsoever of the grantor, either in law or equity, of, in, and to the above bargained premises, with the hereditaments and appurtenances.

TO HAVE AND TO HOLD the said premises above bargained and described, with the appurtenances, unto the grantee, his heirs and assigns forever. And the grantor, for himself, his heirs and personal representatives, does covenant, grant, bargain, and agree to and with the grantee, his heirs and assigns, that at the time of the ensealing and delivery of these presents, he is well seized of the premises above conveyed, has good, sure, perfect, absolute, and indefeasible estate of inheritance, in law, in fee simple, and has good right, full power, and lawful authority to grant, bargain, sell, and convey the same in manner and form as aforesaid, and that the same are free and clear from all former and other grants, bar~ains, sales, liens, taxes, assessments, encumbrances, and restrictions of whatever kind or nature soever, except general taxes for 1994 and subsequent years; except easements, restrictions, covenants, conditions, reservations, and rights of way of record, if any;

      <u>None noted.</u>

The grantor shall and will **WARRANT AND FOREVER DEFEND** the above-bargained premises in the quiet and peaceable possession of the grantee, his heirs assigns, against all and every person or persons lawfully claiming the whole or any part thereof. The singular number shall include the plural, the plural the singular, and the use of any gender shall be applicable to all genders.

IN WITNESS WHEREOF the grantor has executed this deed on the date set forth above.

_____ Seal   _____

Your Name   Witness

_____ Seal   _____

Co-Grantor   Witness

<u>Personal Notary:</u>

State of _____, County of _____.

I, _____, a Notary Public for the County and State aforesaid, do hereby certify that _____ personally appeared before me this day and duly acknowledged the execution of the foregoing instrument.

     Witness my hand and official seal, this the _____ day of _____, 19_____,

_____ . My commission expires _____, 19_____.

(Notary Public)

<u>Corporate notary</u>

State of _____, County of _____.

    I, _____, a Notary Public for the County and State aforesaid, do hereby certify that _____ personally appeared before me this day and duly acknowledged that __he is the Secretary of _____, a _____ Corporation, and that by authority duly given and as the act of the corporation, the foregoing instrument was signed in its name by its President, sealed with its corporate seal, and attested by its Secretary.

    Witness my hand and official seal, this the _____ day of _____, 19____.

_____

(Notary Public)

My commission expires _____, 19____.

                    ****

For official use only

State of _____, County of _____.

    Each of the foregoing certificates, namely of _____ _____, a Notary or Notaries Public of the State and County designated, is certified to be correct.

    This _____ day of _____, 19____.

_____

Register of Deeds, _____ County, by:

_____

Filed for registration on the _____ day of _____, 19____ at

_____ .m.

_____

Register of Deeds, _____ County, by: _____

---

8. CONTRACTS FOR DEED

Contract for Deed When Buying

When recorded, return to:
«First name» «Last name»
«Street»
«City», «State» «Zip code»

Prepared by Your Name   Space above for recorder's use

State of «PropState»   County of «County»

THIS contract for deed, dated «NoteDate», is between the Party of the First Part, known as

«First name» «Last name»
«Cosigner»
«Street»
«City», «State» «Zip code»

and

Your Company Name
Your Address
City, St Zip

also called Party of the Second Part;

WITNESSETH:

That subject to the terms and conditions hereinafter set out, party of the first part has contracted to sell to party of the second part; and party of the second part has contracted to purchase from said party of the first part; a certain tract of land situated in the County of «County» and State of «PropState», such tract of land being more particularly described as follows:

«Legal»

which is also known by this address: «Property».

Initials: _____ _____

The terms and conditions of the sale are as follows:

(1) It is agreed that the purchase price shall be $«SellPrice», payable with a cash down payment of $«DownPmt», [x] subject to [ ] assumption of an existing mortgage of $«BankMtg», and the balance of $«FaceAmt» to be financed by the seller with the following terms: Payable in monthly installments of $«Payment» each, said installments to bear interest at the rate of «Rate» percent per annum on the unpaid balance and to be credited as received first to interest and the balance to principal, beginning on «PmtDate» and continuing on the same day each month. At such time as the entire purchase price has been paid in full, but no later than «Maturity», party of the first part will execute to the party of the second part a good and sufficient warranty deed conveying the above described property and clear of all liens and encumbrances with the exception of standard utility service easements, road rights of way of record, the restriction that no additional right of way shall be granted across this property, and taxes for the year in which the deed is made.

If this contract is subject to an existing mortgage given by the party of the first part, the party of the first part specifically agrees to continue making timely payments; however, upon failure to make timely payments by party of the first part, party of the second part may make the payment directly to the mortgagee and deduct the amount of said payment from the amount owed to the party of the first part.

(2) In addition to the monthly installments above set forth, the party of the second part agrees to pay an additional sum of $«Escrow» per month, said sum to be held in escrow by the party of the first part and to be used for payment of ad valorem real property taxes and insurance premiums for the policy insuring the dwelling on the above described property. Should the amount of taxes and/or insurance premiums increase during the term of this contract, party of the second part will pay such additional sum as may be necessary each month in order to pay these items in full as they come due. During the term of this contract, taxes on said land are to be listed by the party of the first part but paid by the party of the second part from the escrow money as set forth above.

(3) So long as this contract remains in full force and effect, the party of the second part may have the use of the above described land.

(4) If payment is received more than «GraceDays» after the date due, a late fee of $«LateFee» will be added to the monthly amount owed. It is, however, understood and agreed that if any of the said monthly payments, as set forth above, remain overdue and unpaid for a period of more than thirty (30) days, the party of the first part may, at its option, declare the entire unpaid balance due and payable in full immediately. In that event, if said entire remaining balance is not paid within thirty (30) days, this contract shall terminate and be considered null and

Initials: _____ _____

void, and all sums paid by the party of the second part shall be considered as rental on the above described property.

(5) Party of the second part contracts and agrees that the above described property will be maintained in good condition during the term of this contract and the party of the first part shall have no obligation whatsoever for repair or maintenance of said property.

(6) Should the above described property suffer a casualty loss from fire or other similar circumstance during the term of this contract to the extent that the dwelling house located thereon is totally destroyed, the party of the first part shall be entitled to such portion of the insurance proceeds as is required as of the date of said loss to pay the balance of the purchase price for the property in full, and the party of the second part shall be entitled to any sums over and above the amount necessary to pay said contract purchase price in full. Should this event occur and should the outstanding balance be paid in full from the proceeds of the casualty insurance, then and in that event the party of the first part will convey the above described tract to the party of the second part.

(7) Each of the parties hereto further contract and agree that this contract for deed is not assignable, and should the party of the second part convey all or any part of the above described property, or an interest therein, during the term of this contract, then and in that event the entire remaining outstanding balance due under the terms of this contract shall become immediately payable in full. If said sums are not then paid in full, the contract shall become null and void as set forth above.

(8) This agreement is a legal instrument. You should consult your legal or tax advisor before signing this agreement.

(9) Borrower acknowledges receipt of a copy of this contract for deed.

WITNESS our hands and seals, April 15, 2006.

_____ Seal   _____

Buyer: Your Name   Witness

_____ Seal   _____

Buyer: Cosigner   Witness

Initials: _____ _____

_____ Seal   _____

Seller: «First name» «Last name»   Witness

_____ Seal   _____

Seller: «Cosigner»   Witness

<u>Personal Notary:</u>

State of _____, County of _____.

I, _____, a Notary Public for the County and State aforesaid, do hereby certify that _____ personally appeared before me this day and duly acknowledged the execution of the foregoing instrument.

Witness my hand and official seal, this the _____ day of _____, 20____,

_____ . My commission expires _____, 20____.

(Notary Public)

<u>Corporate notary</u>

State of _____, County of _____.

I, _____, a Notary Public for the County and State aforesaid, do hereby certify that _____ personally appeared before me this day and duly acknowledged that __he is the Secretary of _____, a _____ Corporation, and that by authority duly given and as the act of the corporation, the foregoing instrument was signed in its name by its President, sealed with its corporate seal, and attested by its Secretary.

Witness my hand and official seal, this the _____ day of _____, 20____.

_____

(Notary Public)

My commission expires _____, 20____.

****

Initials: _____ _____

For official use only

State of _____, County of _____.

      Each of the foregoing certificates, namely of _____
_____, a Notary or Notaries Public of the State and County
designated, is certified to be correct.

      This _____ day of _____, 20_____.

_____

Register of Deeds, _____ County, by: _____

Filed for registration on the _____ day of _____, 20_____ at
_____ .m.

_____

Register of Deeds, _____ County, by: _____

                                          Initials: _____ _____

Contract for Deed When Selling

When recorded, return to:
Your name
Address
City, State zipcode

Prepared by Your Name   Space above for recorder's use

State of <u>«PropState»</u>   County of <u>«County»</u>

THIS contract for deed, dated <u>«NoteDate»</u>, is between the Party of the First Part, known as

<u>Your Company Name</u>
<u>Your Address</u>
<u>City, St Zip</u>

and

<u>«First name» «Last name»</u>
<u>«Cosigner»</u>
<u>«Street»</u>
<u>«City», «State» «Zip code»</u>

also called Party of the Second Part;

WITNESSETH:

That subject to the terms and conditions hereinafter set out, party of the first part has contracted to sell to party of the second part; and party of the second part has contracted to purchase from said party of the first part; a certain tract of land situated in the County of <u>«County»</u> and State of <u>«PropState»</u>, such tract of land being more particularly described as follows:

«Legal»

which is also known by this address: <u>«Property»</u>.

The terms and conditions of the sale are as follows:

Initials: _____   _____

(1) It is agreed that the purchase price shall be $«SellPrice», payable with a cash down payment of $«DownPmt», [x] subject to [ ] assumption of an existing mortgage of $«BankMtg», and the balance of $«FaceAmt»to be financed by the seller with the following terms: Payable in monthly installments of $«Payment» each, said installments to bear interest at the rate of «Rate» percent per annum on the unpaid balance and to be credited as received first to interest and the balance to principal, beginning on «PmtDate» and continuing on the same day each month. At such time as the entire purchase price has been paid in full, but no later than «Maturity», party of the first part will execute to the party of the second part a good and sufficient warranty deed conveying the above described property and clear of all liens and encumbrances with the exception of standard utility service easements, road rights of way of record, the restriction that no additional right of way shall be granted across this property, and taxes for the year in which the deed is made.

If this contract is subject to an existing mortgage given by the party of the first part, the party of the first part specifically agrees to continue making timely payments; however, upon failure to make timely payments by party of the first part, party of the second part may make the payment directly to the mortgagee and deduct the amount of said payment from the amount owed to the party of the first part.

(2) In addition to the monthly installments above set forth, the party of the second part agrees to pay an additional sum of $«Escrow» per month, said sum to be held in escrow by the party of the first part and to be used for payment of ad valorem real property taxes and insurance premiums for the policy insuring the dwelling on the above described property. Should the amount of taxes and/or insurance premiums increase during the term of this contract, party of the second part will pay such additional sum as may be necessary each month in order to pay these items in full as they come due. During the term of this contract, taxes on said land are to be listed by the party of the first part but paid by the party of the second part from the escrow money as set forth above.

(3) So long as this contract remains in full force and effect, the party of the second part may have the use of the above described land.

(4) If payment is received more than «GraceDays» after the date due, a late fee of $«LateFee» will be added to the monthly amount owed. It is, however, understood and agreed that if any of the said monthly payments, as set forth above, remain overdue and unpaid for a period of more than thirty (30) days, the party of the first part may, at its option, declare the entire unpaid balance due and payable in full immediately. In that event, if said entire remaining balance is not paid within thirty (30) days, this contract shall terminate and be considered null and void, and all sums paid by the party of the second part shall be considered as rental on the above described property.

Initials: _____ _____

(5) Party of the second part contracts and agrees that the above described property will be maintained in good condition during the term of this contract and the party of the first part shall have no obligation whatsoever for repair or maintenance of said property.

(6) Should the above described property suffer a casualty loss from fire or other similar circumstance during the term of this contract to the extent that the dwelling house located thereon is totally destroyed, the party of the first part shall be entitled to such portion of the insurance proceeds as is required as of the date of said loss to pay the balance of the purchase price for the property in full, and the party of the second part shall be entitled to any sums over and above the amount necessary to pay said contract purchase price in full. Should this event occur and should the outstanding balance be paid in full from the proceeds of the casualty insurance, then and in that event the party of the first part will convey the above described tract to the party of the second part.

(7) Each of the parties hereto further contract and agree that this contract for deed is not assignable, and should the party of the second part convey all or any part of the above described property, or an interest therein, during the term of this contract. then and in that event the entire remaining outstanding balance due under the terms of this contract shall become immediately payable in full. If said sums are not then paid in full, the contract shall become null and void as set forth above.

(8) This agreement is a legal instrument. You should consult your legal or tax advisor before signing this agreement.

(9) Borrower acknowledges receipt of a copy of this contract for deed.

WITNESS my hand and seal, April 15, 2006.

_____ Seal   _____

Buyer: «First name» «Last name»   Witness

_____ Seal   _____

Buyer: «Cosigner»   Witness

_____ Seal   _____

Seller: Your Name   Witness

Initials: _____ _____

_____ Seal   _____

Seller: Cosigner   Witness

Personal Notary:

State of _____, County of _____.

I, _____, a Notary Public for the County and State aforesaid, do hereby certify that _____ personally appeared before me this day and duly acknowledged the execution of the foregoing instrument.

      Witness my hand and official seal, this the _____ day of _____, 20_____,

_____ . My commission expires _____, 20_____.

(Notary Public)

Corporate notary

State of _____, County of _____.

      I, _____, a Notary Public for the County and State aforesaid, do hereby certify that _____ personally appeared before me this day and duly acknowledged that __he is the Secretary of _____, a _____ Corporation, and that by authority duly given and as the act of the corporation, the foregoing instrument was signed in its name by its President, sealed with its corporate seal, and attested by its Secretary.

      Witness my hand and official seal, this the _____ day of _____, 20_____.

_____

(Notary Public)

My commission expires _____, 20_____.

                            ****

For official use only

State of _____, County of _____.

      Each of the foregoing certificates, namely of _____ _____, a Notary or Notaries Public of the State and County designated, is certified to be correct.

                                    Initials: _____ _____

This _____ day of _____, 20_____.

_____

Register of Deeds, _____ County, by:

_____

Filed for registration on the _____ day of _____, 20_____ at _____ .m.

_____

Register of Deeds, _____ County, by: _____

Initials: _____ _____

9. FORECLOSURE MARKETING LETTER

Your Company Name
123 Main Street
Anywhere, USA 00000
(123) 456-7890

April 15, 2006

«Title» «First name» «Last name»
«Company»
«Street»
«City», «State» «Zip code»

Re: First deed of trust and note
        Security: «Property»

Dear «Title» «Last name»,

I am inquiring about purchasing the above referenced property for my own use.

If you would like to sell this property, please contact me at your earliest convenience.

Sincerely,

Your Name

10. OPEN HOUSE SAMPLE MARKETING SHEETS

Home for Sale

This beautiful, executive style home is available for $100,000. The owner is willing to hold financing with a reasonable down payment.

The home features 4 bedrooms, 3 baths, and a 2 car garage. It is conveniently located to Shepardson Elementary School, Scotch Pines Shopping Center, and the city bus line.

For an appointment or to discuss your offer with the owner, call Lisa at 123-456-7890.

Features of this home

Square footage	1,760	Electric	$35
BR/BA/Gar	4/3/2	Gas	.40
Heat	Forced air gas	Water	.25
Built	1984	Trash, other utilities	.20
Roof	1984	Taxes 1995	.890
Furnace	1994	Insurance 1995	.320
Hot water heater	1996	Assessments	.0

Home for Rent

This beautiful, executive style home is available for $845 rent per month to qualified tenants. Before moving in, you must pay the first month and security deposit in advance, which will be a total of $1,790 in cash, money order, or certified funds. The owner requires a credit application.

The home is large enough for a family of 5. You may have up to two household pets for an additional $10 each per month.

The home features 4 bedrooms, 3 baths, and a 2 car garage. It is conveniently located to Shepardson Elementary School, Scotch Pines Shopping Center, and the city bus line.

For an appointment to discuss this property with the owner, call Lisa at 123-456-7890.

Features of this home

Square footage	1,760	Electric	$35
BR/BA/Gar	4/3/2	Gas	.40
Heat	Forced air gas	Water	.25
Built	1984	Trash, other utilities	.20

11. BASIC OPTION AGREEMENTS

Basic Option Agreement for Buying Property

When recorded, return to:
Your Name
Address
City, St Zipcode

Prepared by Your Name   Space above for recorder's use

For $10.00 and other considerations paid to

<u>Your Name</u>

otherwise known as the Seller, the receipt and sufficiency of which are hereby acknowledged, the Seller hereby gives and grants to

<u>«First name» «Last name»</u>
<u>«Cosigner»</u>

otherwise known as Purchaser, the exclusive option to purchase the property, together with all improvements thereon, known as

<u>«Property»</u>

situated in the County of <u>«County»</u>.

If Purchaser decides to purchase the property, Purchaser must notify Seller on or before <u>«Maturity»</u>, which notice must be in writing and sent by registered or certified mail or delivered personally.

The total purchase price of the property shall be $<u>«SellPrice»</u>, which shall be paid as follows:

Down payment . . . .«DownPmt»
Funds from new bank mortgage . . . .«BankMtg»
New purchase money mortgage . . . .«SellerMtg»
Other financing . . . .«OtherMtg»

Initials: _____ _____

If the option is not exercised on or before the above date, the option money paid hereunder WILL NOT BE REFUNDED to Purchaser.

In the event the option is exercised, the property will be transferred and the closing will take place upon the following terms and conditions:

1. Purchase price. The purchase price will include all fixtures currently on the premises, together with all built-in appliances, all window coverings, and all wall-to-wall carpeting, all in their present condition, free and clear of all encumbrances.

2. Title. If title is not merchantable, the Purchaser may demand and receive the return of the option money paid hereunder.

3. Title insurance. Seller will furnish a title insurance policy to the Purchaser after the closing and pay the premium thereon.

4. Taxes. Taxes, as determined by the current levy and assessment, and all prepaid items, shall be apportioned to the date of closing when the deed and possession of the property shall be delivered to Purchaser.

5. Closing. The time and place of closing shall be designated by the Seller, who shall convey merchantable title by a good and sufficient general warranty deed, at such time free and clear of all taxes and encumbrances except:

Property taxes due and payable at the end of the current year

6. Default. In the event of a default hereunder by the Purchaser, Seller shall be entitled to keep the option money without accounting to Purchaser therefor. In the event Seller defaults under the terms and conditions hereof, the Purchaser may demand and receive the return of the option money paid hereunder, or may have the right to an action for specific performance of this contract. In the event a civil action is filed regarding the terms of this contract, the prevailing party shall be entitled to recover all costs and expenses, including reasonable attorney's fees.

WITNESS my hand and seal, April 15, 2006.

_____ Seal   _____

Buyer: Your Name   Witness

                                              Initials: _____   _____

_____ Seal   _____

Buyer: Cosigner   Witness

_____ Seal   _____

Seller: «First name» «Last name»   Witness

_____ Seal   _____

Seller: «Cosigner»   Witness

Personal notary:

State of _____, County of _____.

I, _____, a Notary Public for the County and State aforesaid, do hereby certify that _____ personally appeared before me this day and duly acknowledged the execution of the foregoing instrument.

      Witness my hand and official seal, this the _____ day of _____, 20_____,

_____ . My commission expires _____, 20_____.

(Notary Public)

Corporate notary

State of _____, County of _____.

      I, _____, a Notary Public for the County and State aforesaid, do hereby certify that _____ personally appeared before me this day and duly acknowledged that __he is the Secretary of _____, a _____ Corporation, and that by authority duly given and as the act of the corporation, the foregoing instrument was signed in its name by its President, sealed with its corporate seal, and attested by its Secretary.

      Witness my hand and official seal, this the _____ day of _____, 20_____.

_____

(Notary Public)

My commission expires _____, 20_____.

                        ****

                                            Initials: _____   _____

For official use only

State of _____, County of _____.

     Each of the foregoing certificates, namely of _____
_____, a Notary or Notaries Public of the State and County
designated, is certified to be correct.

     This _____ day of _____, 20_____.

_____

Register of Deeds,_____ County, by: _____

Filed for registration on the _____ day of _____, 20_____ at
_____ .m.

_____

Register of Deeds, _____ County, by: _____

                                 Initials: _____ _____

Basic Option Agreement for Selling a Lease

When recorded, return to:
«First name» «Last name»
«Street»
«City», «State» «Zip code»

Prepared by Your Name   Space above for recorder's use

For $10.00 and other considerations paid to

<u>Your Name</u>

otherwise known as the Seller, the receipt and sufficiency of which are hereby acknowledged, the Seller hereby gives and grants to

<u>«First name» «Last name»</u>
<u>«Cosigner»</u>

otherwise known as Purchaser, the exclusive option to purchase the property, together with all improvements thereon, known as

<u>«Property»</u>

situated in the County of <u>«County»</u>.

If Purchaser decides to purchase the property, Purchaser must notify Seller on or before <u>«Maturity»</u>, which notice must be in writing and sent by registered or certified mail or delivered personally.

The total purchase price of the property shall be $<u>«SellPrice»</u>, which shall be paid as follows:

> Down payment . . . . «DownPmt»
> Funds from new bank mortgage . . . . «BankMtg»
> New purchase money mortgage . . . . «SellerMtg»
> Other financing . . . . «OtherMtg»

If the option is not exercised on or before the above date, the option money paid hereunder WILL NOT BE REFUNDED to Purchaser.

Initials: _____   _____

In the event the option is exercised, the property will be transferred and the closing will take place upon the following terms and conditions:

1. Purchase price. The purchase price will include all fixtures currently on the premises, together with all built-in appliances, all window coverings, and all wall-to-wall carpeting, all in their present condition, free and clear of all encumbrances.

2. Title. If title is not merchantable, the Purchaser may demand and receive the return of the option money paid hereunder.

3. Title insurance. Seller will furnish a title insurance policy to the Purchaser after the closing and pay the premium thereon.

4. Taxes. Taxes, as determined by the current levy and assessment, and all prepaid items, shall be apportioned to the date of closing when the deed and possession of the property shall be delivered to Purchaser.

5. Closing. The time and place of closing shall be designated by the Seller, who shall convey merchantable title by a good and sufficient general warranty deed, at such time free and clear of all taxes and encumbrances except:

Property taxes due and payable at the end of the current year

6. Default. In the event of a default hereunder by the Purchaser, Seller shall be entitled to keep the option money without accounting to Purchaser therefor. In the event Seller defaults under the terms and conditions hereof, the Purchaser may demand and receive the return of the option money paid hereunder, or may have the right to an action for specific performance of this contract. In the event a civil action is filed regarding the terms of this contract, the prevailing party shall be entitled to recover all costs and expenses, including reasonable attorney's fees.

WITNESS my hand and seal, April 15, 2006.

_____ Seal   _____

Seller: Your Name   Witness

_____ Seal   _____

Seller: Cosigner   Witness

Initials: _____   _____

_____ Seal   _____

Buyer: «First name» «Last name»   Witness

_____ Seal   _____

Buyer: «Cosigner»   Witness

Personal notary:

State of _____, County of _____.

I, _____, a Notary Public for the County and State aforesaid, do hereby certify that _____ personally appeared before me this day and duly acknowledged the execution of the foregoing instrument.

Witness my hand and official seal, this the _____ day of _____, 20_____,

_____ . My commission expires _____, 20_____.

(Notary Public)

Corporate notary

State of _____, County of _____.

I, _____, a Notary Public for the County and State aforesaid, do hereby certify that _____ personally appeared before me this day and duly acknowledged that __he is the Secretary of _____, a _____ Corporation, and that by authority duly given and as the act of the corporation, the foregoing instrument was signed in its name by its President, sealed with its corporate seal, and attested by its Secretary.

Witness my hand and official seal, this the _____ day of _____, 20_____.

_____

(Notary Public)

My commission expires _____, 20_____.

****

Initials: _____ _____

For official use only

State of _____, County of _____.

       Each of the foregoing certificates, namely of _____
_____, a Notary or Notaries Public of the State and County
designated, is certified to be correct.

       This _____ day of _____, 20_____.

_____

Register of Deeds, _____ County, by: _____

Filed for registration on the _____ day of _____, 20_____ at
_____ .m.

_____

Register of Deeds, _____ County, by: _____

                                       Initials: _____ _____

                                       Initials: _____ _____

12. POWER OF ATTORNEY

When recorded, return to:
Your Name
Address
City, St Zipcode

Prepared by Your Name   Space above for recorder's use

KNOW ALL MEN BY THESE PRESENTS, that I, <u>Principal's Name</u>, of the county of <u>County</u>, state of <u>State</u>, reposing special trust and confidence in <u>Attorney Name</u>, have made, constituted, and appointed this person my true and lawful attorney to act for me and in my name, place, and stead, and for my sole use and benefit, with full power and authority to do and perform each and every act necessary, as fully as I might do if personally present, to accomplish and complete the following to wit:

<u>Specific action to complete or unlimited actions</u>
<u>Date of expiration or expires on completing actions above</u>
<u>Effective upon, or not affected by, the disability of the principal</u>

WITNESS my hand and seal, April 15, 2006.

_____ (Seal)

Your Name

_____ (Seal)

Witness

_____ (Seal)

Witness

* * * * * * *

Personal Notary:

State of _____, County of _____.

I, _____, a Notary Public for the County and State aforesaid, do hereby certify that _____ personally appeared before me this day and duly acknowledged the execution of the foregoing instrument.

  Witness my hand and official seal, this the _____ day of _____, 20_____,

_____ . My commission expires _____, 20_____.

(Notary Public)

13. RENTAL APPLICATION

Property: _____   Unit: _____

Name of applicant: _____   SSN and Driver's License: _____
Spouse or Roommate: _____   SSN and Driver's License: _____

Children's names and ages: _____   _____
_____   _____
Names of other occupants: _____   Relationship: _____
Pets: _____   Kind: _____

Present address: _____   Phone: _____
Amount of rent: _____   How long: _____
Manager's name:_____   Manager's phone: _____

Previous residence:_____   _____
Amount of rent: _____   How long: _____
Manager's name:_____   Manager's phone: _____

Employment information:
Employer: _____   Employer phone: _____
Address:_____   Monthly salary: _____
_____   How long: _____

Spouse or roommate employment information:
Employer: _____   Employer phone: _____
Address:_____   Monthly salary: _____
_____   How long: _____

Financial information:
Bank and branch: _____   Phone : _____
Saving account: _____   Checking account: _____
Other accounts:_____   Other assets: _____
Major credit cards: _____   Number: _____

Monthly obligations:
Car:_____   Balance and payment: _____
Child support and alimony:_____   Balance and payment: _____
Other:_____   Balance and payment: _____
Other:_____   Balance and payment: _____

Automobiles:
Make, model, year: _____ License: _____
Make, model, year: _____ License: _____

Personal references:
Name: _____ Phone: _____
Name: _____ Phone: _____

In case of emergency notify:
_____ Relationship: _____
Address: _____ Phone: _____

Personal skills:
[ ] Plumbing   [ ] Carpentry   [ ] Painting   [ ] Roofing   [ ] Electrical   [ ] Mechanical   [ ]

Other: _____

Are there any outstanding judgments against any resident?	[ ] Yes [ ] No
Have you ever been evicted from any tenancy?	[ ] Yes [ ] No
Have you ever willfully and intentionally refused to pay rent when due?	[ ] Yes [ ] No
Do you know of anything that may interrupt your income or ability to pay?	[ ] Yes [ ] No
Have you ever filed a petition for bankruptcy?	[ ] Yes [ ] No

I understand that if I do not live up to the terms of the lease, or fail to pay the rent, information may be turned over to a credit reporting agency. Only those listed above will occupy the premises. I HEREBY AUTHORIZE YOU TO OBTAIN A CREDIT BUREAU REPORT AND I AGREE TO PAY THE REQUESTED FEE FOR THIS SERVICE. I certify that the asnwers I have given in this application are true and correct to the best of my knowledge. Any false answers or statements made by me will be sufficient grounds for eviction and loss of deposits.

Date:

_____   _____
Applicant's signature   Co-applicant's signature

14. SATISFACTIONS OF DEBT

Satisfaction of Debt When Paying off a Debt

When recorded, return to:
Your name
Address
City, State Zipcode

Prepared by Your Name   Space above for recorder's use

THIS AGREEMENT, dated April 15, 2006, is between:

Your Company Name
Your Address
City, St Zip

also called the party of the first part, and:

«First name» «Last name»
«Cosigner»
«Street»
«City», «State» «Zip code»

also called the party of the second part.

Both parties covenant and agree as follows, that in fulfillment of the obligation of the party of the first part, namely, the note and mortgage/deed of trust in the original amount of $«FaceAmt», dated «NoteDate», recorded in «NoteRec» of the records of «County» County, State of «PropState», the party of the second part fully and absolutely releases the party of the first part from any and all obligations now and in the future from the above named note and mortgage/deed of trust and fully and absolutely releases, cancels, and forever discharges said mortgage/deed of trust.

WITNESS our hands and seals, April 15, 2006.

_____ Seal   _____

«First name» «Last name»   Witness

_____ Seal   _____

«Cosigner»   Witness

Personal Notary:

State of _____, County of _____.

I, _____, a Notary Public for the County and State aforesaid, do hereby certify that _____ personally appeared before me this day and duly acknowledged the execution of the foregoing instrument.

     Witness my hand and official seal, this the _____ day of _____, 20_____,

_____ . My commission expires _____, 20_____.

(Notary Public)

Corporate notary

State of _____, County of _____.

     I, _____, a Notary Public for the County and State aforesaid, do hereby certify that _____ personally appeared before me this day and duly acknowledged that __he is the Secretary of _____, a _____ Corporation, and that by authority duly given and as the act of the corporation, the foregoing instrument was signed in its name by its President, sealed with its corporate seal, and attested by its Secretary.

     Witness my hand and official seal, this the _____ day of _____, 20_____.

_____

(Notary Public)

My commission expires _____, 20_____.

               ****

For official use only

State of _____, County of _____.

     Each of the foregoing certificates, namely of _____ _____, a Notary or Notaries Public of the State and County designated, is certified to be correct.

     This _____ day of _____, 20_____.

Register of Deeds, _____ County, by: _____

Filed for registration on the _____ day of _____, 20_____ at _____ .m.

Register of Deeds, _____ County, by: _____

Satisfaction of Debt When Being Paid a Debt

When recorded, return to:
«First name» «Last name»
«Street»
«City», «State» «Zip code»

Prepared by Your Name   Space above for recorder's use

THIS AGREEMENT, dated April 15, 2006, is between:

«First name» «Last name»
«Cosigner»
«Street»
«City», «State» «Zip code»

also called the party of the first part, and:

Your Company Name
Your Address
City, St Zip

also called the party of the second part.

Both parties covenant and agree as follows, that in fulfillment of the obligation of the party of the first part, namely, the note and mortgage/deed of trust in the original amount of $«FaceAmt», dated «NoteDate», recorded in «NoteRec» of the records of «County» County, State of «PropState», the party of the second part releases the party of the first part from any and all obligations now and in the future from the above named note and mortgage/deed of trust and fully and absolutely releases, cancels, and forever discharges said mortgage/deed of trust.

WITNESS our hands and seals, April 15, 2006.

_____ Seal   _____

Your Name   Witness

_____ Seal   _____

Cosigner   Witness

Personal Notary:

State of _____, County of _____.

I, _____, a Notary Public for the County and State aforesaid, do hereby certify that _____ personally appeared before me this day and duly acknowledged the execution of the foregoing instrument.

Witness my hand and official seal, this the _____ day of _____, 20_____,

_____ . My commission expires _____, 20_____.

(Notary Public)

Corporate notary

State of _____, County of _____.

I, _____, a Notary Public for the County and State aforesaid, do hereby certify that _____ personally appeared before me this day and duly acknowledged that __he is the Secretary of _____, a _____ Corporation, and that by authority duly given and as the act of the corporation, the foregoing instrument was signed in its name by its President, sealed with its corporate seal, and attested by its Secretary.

Witness my hand and official seal, this the _____ day of _____, 20_____.

_____

(Notary Public)

My commission expires _____, 20_____.

****

For official use only

State of _____, County of _____.

Each of the foregoing certificates, namely of _____ _____, a Notary or Notaries Public of the State and County designated, is certified to be correct.

This _____ day of _____, 20_____.

Register of Deeds, _____ County, by: _____

Filed for registration on the _____ day of _____, 20_____ at _____ .m.

Register of Deeds, _____ County, by: _____

15. TESTIMONIAL LETTER

Your Company Name
123 Main Street
Anywhere, USA 00000
(123) 456-7890

April 15, 2006

«Title» «First name» «Last name»
«Company»
«Street»
«City», «State» «Zip code»

Dear «Title» «Last name»,

You recently completed a financial transaction with our company. Please answer the following questions below so that we can improve our service for future customers. Thank you for your help.

1. How would you rate us?

2. Was the transaction satisfactory to you?

3. Would you recommend our company to others who need our service?

4. May we use this letter to show other potential clients?

5. Your signature:

Sincerely,

Your Name

16. MISCELLANEOUS CLAUSES

This file contains miscellaneous clauses that can be copied and pasted into various documents. Some are better when you are buying, while others should only be used when you sell.

Prepayment. Payor may prepay 12 monthly payments during the month of January in exchange for the beneficiary accepting the entire sum reduced by 15%. [Ask for 15%, settle for 10% or even 5%. Any discount you get for prepayment will double your yield over a 12-month period. Try it with a calculator. And your risk is reduced. There may be some tax ramifications if you are paying a mortgage, since you are getting debt relief, but it is worth it.]

Right of First Refusal. Option is given to the borrower to pay off this note if lender should decide to sell, discount, or assign this note; borrower may pay off this note at the same terms as the proposed sale, discount, or assignment within 30 days of receiving written notice; and further, lender shall not sell, discount, or assign said note without prior written approval of the borrower. [Wouldn't you hate to set up a good seller financed transaction and then have someone else share? Buying back your own debt is one of the best wealth builders available to the typical investor—especially if you can buy it at a discount.]

Payment. The sum of $10,000.00 together with interest at the rate of 10% per annum, said principal and interest payable in monthly installments of $132.15 or more, with the first payment being due August 13, 1996, and successive payments being due on the 13th of each month following. [Do not state this as 120 monthly payments, because it is not the 120 payments, but the $132.15, that will amortize this loan. Also, emphasize "or more" to improve cash flow and reduce risk. If you are making the payments, try to get the first payment due date 90 days after closing to improve your cash flow. Finally, payments can be due on any day of the month, but remember February does not have 30 or 31 days—ever.]

Payment. The first 12 installments are due in the amount of $500.00 each, the next 12 installments are due in the amount of $550.00, and the remaining payments are due in the amount of $600.00. [This will help you get a cash-strapped, but promising, payor into your property. As a payor, use this technique to push cash outflows back until you can raise the rents to pay it easily.]

Application of payments. Payments will be applied first to escrow for taxes and insurance, then to any fees advanced by the mortgagee, then to any late fees outstanding, then to interest owed to the date the payment is made, and finally to reduce the principal balance. [This is the best order if you are receiving payments, since the first items paid normally do not bear interest. Also, "interest owed to date" implies interest will be calculated daily, which eliminates the float of a grace period.]

Application of payments. Payments will be applied first to escrow for taxes and insurance, then to periodic interest owed to the date due, then to any fees advanced by the mortgagee, then to any late fees outstanding, and finally to reduce the principal balance. [This is a better sequence if you are paying. It is standard practice that escrow be taken first, since the mortgagee has an obligation to pay taxes and insurance if the mortgagee is responsible to collect escrow. The term "periodic interest" implies checking the payment off of an amortization schedule, so you benefit from the float granted by the grace period. These tips will net you a few dollars over the course of a loan, but remember that if your goal is to avoid making payments, you are in the wrong business and on the wrong planet.]

Wraparound note. This contract is subject to an existing mortgage given by the party of the first part. The party of the first part specifically agrees to continue making timely payments; however, upon failure to make timely payments by party of the first part, party of the second part may make the payment directly to the underlying mortgagee and deduct the amount of said payment from the amount owed to the party of the first part. [This is a minor protection for the party purchasing the property. If you are the purchaser, look for a future advance clause in the underlying, which could wipe out your equity, and have the payor sign a waiver of future advance. Make sure that your payments are sufficient for the seller to make payments on the underlying. We saw one case where the seller was making small, interest only payments with a balloon due at the end, while the buyer was making large, fully amortizing payments. As long as the seller saved the difference each month to make the balloon payment—well, need we say more?]

Time is of the essence. It is agreed that time is of the essence of this agreeement and that in the event of default in payment of any installment for a period of 45 days, the holder of this note may declare all the remainder of said debt due and collectible. [Go for 5 days if you are collecting, 45 or more if you are paying.]

Time is of the essence. It is agreed that time is of the essence of this agreeement and that in the event of default in payment of any installment for a period of 30 days, the holder of this note may declare all the remainder of said debt, including accrued and unpaid interest, due and collectible without notice, and such sum shall bear interest at the highest rate allowed by law. [Using "highest rate" allows you to collect more than the face rate of the note and, if the law changes, the maximum rate wherever the state may set it. Be careful of charging interest on accrued interest, since some states may use that profit when calculating your yield, which then may be usurious. Also, some states prohibit charging any interest on interest. These are referred to as USRule states.]

Prepayment. Option is given to the borrower to pay more or the entire principal balance remaining at any time without penalty, with interest to date of payment only. This is normal.

Prepayment. Borrower may not prepay the entire principal balance during the first 5 years following the signing of this note. [Sellers with huge equity will want to pay taxes over a period of years on the installment method. Prepayment aggravates mortgagees with large tax bills, although if you want to do your part for America, it does please the IRS.]

Prepayment. Option is given to the borrower to pay the entire principal balance remaining at any time; however, mortgagee will accept a 10% discount for a complete payoff within 5 years. [If you can pay a 10% late penalty, why not a 10% early bonus?]

Security. The property securing this note shall be the sole security for this obligation, and the borrower shall in no event be personally liable. [If the seller refuses to allow this, you have to wonder how secure the security really is. Some state law mandates this clause anyway, but there are states that allow for personal liability and deficiency judgments. Watch out!]

Substitution of collateral. Borrower shall have the right at any time to substitute the mortgage given to secure this obligation using any other mortgage on real property, or other collateral acceptable to the Mortgagee, in which borrower can demonstrate that the equity in such substituted collateral is at least as great as the current equity in this mortgaged property, in which event Mortgagee shall properly execute a satisfaction of this mortgage. [Use this to work toward consolidating debt on some properties and releasing others from their debt. A few years ago investors were offering government bonds, which may have a greater inherent worth to some mortgagees.]

Future advance. Upon request by Borrower and at Lender's option within 20 years from the date of this mortgage, Lender may make future advances to Borrower. Such future advance, with interest, shall be secured by this mortgage when evidenced by promissory notes stating that said notes are secured hereby. At no time shall the principal amount of the indebtedness secured by this mortgage exceed the original amount of the note plus $50,000.00. [The amount of the advance is negotiable, as are the terms on succeeding promissory notes. This allows additional funds to be advanced without jeopardizing junior lien holders, since the advance is specified here. Adjusting the terms of a mortgage materially can trigger all the taxes on an otherwise installment sale. Also, when jeopardizing junior lien holders, they can protest in court and actually be allowed to jump ahead of your position.]

Assignment of Rents. As additional security, Borrower assigns to Lender the rents of the property, provided that Borrower shall, prior to acceleration or abandonment of the Property, have the right to collect and retain such rents as they become due and payable. [This will help prevent the borrower from keeping the rents and not paying the mortgage—a quick and dirty technique for improving cash flow.]

Appointment of Receiver. Upon acceleration or abandonment of the Property, Lender shall be entitled to have a receiver appointed by a court to enter upon, take possession of, and manage the Property, and to collect the rents of the Property, including those past due. All rents collected by the receiver shall be applied first to payment of the costs of management of the Property and collection of rents, including, but not limited to, receiver's fees, premiums on receiver's bonds, and reasonable attorney's fees, and then to the sums secured by this Mortgage. The receiver shall be liable to account only for those rents actually received. [When you sell and hold a mortgage, this clause will help prevent a wasting of the property and keep the deadbeat payor from milking the rents and not paying the mortgage.]

Farm animal exclusion. Each of the parties hereto further agrees that no hogs or chickens shall be kept on the above described property and no more than two horses or two cows or any combination thereof shall be kept on the above described property. At such time as the deed to the property is made to the party of the second part, this restriction shall be placed therein.

[Use this in rural or semirural areas so your collateral does not turn into chicken feed. Literally.]

Master Form Mortgage. This mortgage is subject to a Master Form Mortgage. [This means you are reading the "*Reader's Digest*" version of the mortgage. The epic version appears on the county records, and you had better get a copy of it, read it, and agree to it before signing the short form.]

Terms. Wherever used herein, the terms Mortgagor and Mortgagee include all the parties to this instrument, and the heirs, legal representatives, and assigns of individuals, and the successor and assigns of corporations; and the term Note includes all the notes herein described if more than one. Whenever used, the singular number shall include the plural and the plural the singular, and use of any gender shall include all genders. [Legalese for "Don't be too picky."]

Option extension. At the scheduled termination of this option, optionee can extend the term of the option, one time only, for one year with a cash payment of $1,000.00 to optionor.

Release. Upon written request of Borrower, Lender will release portions of the Property upon the payment of $5,000.00 per acre. Lender will credit $2,000.00 of this payment to the next regularly scheduled payment. [The first sentence is standard practice for investors, whom we affectionately call "dirt merchants," when they buy large tracts of land for subdividing and resale. The second sentence will improve your cash flow if you are the payor.]

This document prepared by Your Name and Address. [Many states require this information, so be sure to use your name, not ours. Remember, we set up your computer. Develop a relationship with a local real estate attorney to set up your documents.]

Index

Printed sample forms are provided on pages listed in bold

About the Author

Lisa has been a real estate investor since 1978, a note investor since 1988, and a well-known marketing expert. She has consulted for some of the nation's top financial services industries in private mortgage, business loans, and individual retirement plans.

She has taught over 1,000 workshops and seminars devoted to real estate investing, marketing, and business forums. She is a professional member of the National Speaker's Association and sits on the board of the National Real Estate Investor's Association.

She is currently Marketing Director for The Entrust Group, the nation's largest network of third-party administrators. Entrust provides record-keeping services for individuals who wish to truly self-direct their retirement plans to buy real estate or any alternative investment allowable by the IRS.

Her topic, "Building a Successful Real Estate and Loan Portfolio," will assist any investor, no matter what level of experience they have in real estate or notes. It will also increase investors' knowledge and allow them to take home valuable information and techniques for building wealth.